"As an expert in the area of criminal background searches, Barry not only brings to light the legal aspects of this area, but also brings forward all of the important elements needed in handling background searches appropriately with little to no repercussion to the company. Sleuthing 101, Background Checks and the Law should be on every employer's desk as a 'how to' on criminal background searches."

Brent Houchin
Assistant Manager of Human Resources
Six Flags California

"Employers walk a fine line between protecting their company and employees while avoiding violations of employment law and privacy issues. This booklet provides a simplified guide to conduct sound business practices while avoiding the legal pitfalls of labor law."

Walt Kainz, CPP, CFE
National Director of Corporate Security
Major Health Insurance Company

"Sleuthing 101 is a guide every HR professional, business owner and hiring manager should read before extending that next offer letter. In California, with all the regulations we face and the litigious environment, an employer really needs to be proactive about protecting themselves and their employees from the harm of hiring the wrong person. Barry Nadell has proven to be a tremendous resource as an expert in providing employers the information they need to know to help them make educated and effective hiring decisions."

Jaenene Geiger Maldonado, Consulting Services Manager
The Employers Group

"Sleuthing 101 is an easy read for business owners and leaders in explaining the law and the valid reasons to use background as the initial employment step in an effort to protect both the company and it's employees. I plan to recommend it to all my clients."

Anita Gorino, SPHR, Human Resources Consultant

"Sleuthing 101 is a well-written and comprehensive reference. This book will prove to be a very useful and powerful resource for employers."

Michael Sankey, CEO
BRB Publications

Sleuthing 101: Background Checks and The Law

©2004 by Barry J. Nadell
InfoLink Screening Services, Inc.
9201 Oakdale Avenue, Suite 100
Chatsworth, CA 91311-6520
Phone: (818/800) 990-4473
Fax: (818) 709-2355
www.infolinkscreening.com
www.greathire.com
www.sleuthing101.com
www.barrynadell.com

ISBN: 0-9759372-0-0

Author & Publisher: Barry J. Nadell

Cover Design by: Robin Fox & Associates

Editing and Page Formatting by: Lynne A. Davis and Julie Crawshaw

Printing by: Victor Graphics, Inc.

Second Printing 2005

Cataloging-in-Publication Data
    Nadell, Barry J.
        Sleuthing 101, background checks and the law/author
        & publisher, Barry J. Nadell.
        p. cm.
        ISBN 0-9759372-0-0

        1. Employee screening--United States.   2. Employee
    screening--Law and legislation--United States.
    I. Title.

    HF5549.5.E429N33   658.3'112
                                 QBI04-200517

Acknowledgements

This book is dedicated to my family, friends and clients (many of whom have become good friends). I especially want to thank my wife Leslie, for without her, there would have never been InfoLink Screening Services and there would have never been this book, which she encouraged me to write for two years. Thank you Leslie, your dedication, knowledge, leadership, insight, friendship, caring and love are my inspiration daily.

A special thank you is due to the more than 80 associates at InfoLink, who have dedicated themselves to professionally servicing our clients and helping us to grow. It has been especially gratifying to have associates like Alma, Annel, Cheri, Lalo, Linda, Joe, Shontell, Sonia, Silvia and Sue who have been with InfoLink from five to nine years. Also, I can't forget to thank two important people. First, Dawn Charouhas, my research assistant, who spent many many hours researching law on my behalf for this project and Debi Jamora, my executive assistant who has been with me for over 9 years with her dedication, knowledge, and hard work. In addition, I very much appreciate having a strong management team, for without them, I could not have spent so many hours writing this book.

To those who spent several hours of their personal time reading and offering suggestions to the original manuscripts, thank you. The excellent comments I received from Art Silbergeld, Esq., Eric Joss, Esq., Mike Sanke, Anita Gorino, SPHR, Phil Smith, Pam Lewis and Barry Nixon helped make this book more valuable to employers . . . thank you so much. I owe special thanks to two talented and brilliant friends. First Paul Falcone for dedicating himself to the human resource profession and sharing his knowledge and experience through teaching, articles, speaking and authoring four best selling books with a fifth coming soon; and, W. Barry Nixon who has dedicated his life to stamping out workplace violence and educating employers to hire the very best personnel.

I also feel honored to acknowledge the special relationship I have with the several human resource professionals in Professionals in Human Resources, especially District 9. PIHRA is celebrating its 60th year as one of the largest associations dedicated to the education and professionalism of those in human resources in Southern California. Thank you for allowing me to give back to the industry through my participation on your board for over eight years.

Finally, I can't say enough about the clients I have enjoyed working with. Thank you for allowing InfoLink to partner with you for your background screening, drug testing and employment physicals. Without you, I would not have truly understood just how important background screening is to employers, and I would not have the stories that make this book come to life.

Thank You!
Barry J. Nadell

Employers today must protect themselves and their employees
from the harm of hiring the wrong person.

That is why today they are turning to background checks
on job applicants and employees.

Sleuthing 101 offers an easy to read and understand guide
on the laws surrounding background screening
with examples and stories offered to protect both
the company and its employees.

Sleuthing 101 is a guide every human resources professional,
business owner and hiring manager
should read before extending that next offer letter.

NOTE: Laws described in this
book may have changed. Please
check with your Legal Advisor.

Table of Contents

Preface

Since September 11, 2001, many companies have come to appreciate the value created by background checking companies. In addition, employee theft is said to impact 1% of retailers' revenues year after year—a staggering amount—and falsified employment applications remain a tremendous challenge for most employers. Most of all, violence in the workplace makes headline news all too often, and wouldn't it be great to be able to shield your company from that risk by minimizing the chances that it could happen in your workplace? Hiring new employees without the security provided by performing background checks is no doubt risky in terms of preserving a safe working environment, but it's also problematic in terms of avoiding negligent hiring and retention claims. In short, you'll make a far better record by adding background checks to your hiring program as a critical adjunct to references, tests, and the like.

I've had the pleasure of working with Barry Nadell for ten years and have incorporated InfoLink's services into the companies where I've worked over that same period of time. Barry has guest-lectured in both the Recruitment and the Legal Aspects of Human Resource Management classes that I teach at UCLA Extension, and his knowledge of the law and recognition as a true subject matter expert in this field testifies to his expertise in the discipline of employment background screening. I've watched Barry write bills that have impacted legislation in California, and I wasn't at all surprised to see him interviewed by Peter Jennings on ABC News one night when I was sitting at home watching TV.

Barry's guidance over the years included advising me how to set up InfoLink's program quickly and effectively, how to redraft my company's employment application, how to interpret the findings of complicated cases, and how to deal with adverse action matters. Now that same advice is available to you . . .

Sleuthing 101 is the only work of its kind that combines everything you need to know in one easy to understand format. Simply put, you'll understand the law, legal theory, and more importantly, its practical application in your workplace. You'll have a handy guide and a guiding hand that walks you step-by-step through the implementation process and that will serve as a ready reference for your recruitment and hiring practices. I'm very happy to see that Barry has taken the opportunity to share his knowledge and shed light on this somewhat complex, but oh so critical, subject.

Paul Falcone

Paul Falcone is the author of several best-selling books published by AMACOM including: 101 Sample Write-Ups for Documenting Employee Performance Problems: A Guide to Progressive Discipline and Termination, 96 Great Interview Questions to Ask Before You Hire, and The Hiring and Firing Question and Answer Book. Paul is also regular contributor to HR Magazine, an instructor in UCLA Extension's School of Business and Management, and an internationally recognized speaker in the field of Human Resource Management.

Foreword

The tragic events of September 11, 2001 awakened employers to the critical need to know whom they are hiring and whom they have on their payroll. The threat of making a bad hire moved beyond concerns about minimizing legal liability for negligent hiring and individual incidents or workplace violence to the total new spectrum of mass destruction by terrorism.

Never before have employers received such a wake up call about the need to be proactive in taking all reasonable means necessary to protect their company's assets—their employees, managers, equipment and facilities. That is why today employers are turning to background checking on applicants and employees in record numbers.

Sleuthing 101 offers an easy to read and understandable guide that addresses the full realm of laws that deal with background screening along with examples and stories to easily demonstrate the essential points. Sleuthing 101 provides information that every person involved in the hiring process from human resource professionals, business owners, security professionals, hiring managers, etc. should read and become familiar with. The book is the definitive source of information on background checking and screening that is a must read for anyone involved with background checking in their firm. It should be required reading for all personnel that are directly responsible for handling, reviewing and making decisions regarding background checks for a firm.

No organizations whether large, small, public, private, not for profit, etc. should ever again hire a new employee that has not successfully been screened. The need has clearly been established, the necessary knowledge has been clearly defined in Sleuthing 101, so the only remaining factor is for you to pick up the phone or go online to start checking backgrounds today.

W. Barry Nixon, SPHR
Executive Director,
The National Institute for the Prevention of Workplace Violence, Inc.

About Barry J. Nadell

Barry lives eight minutes from his office in Chatsworth, California. He and his wife, Leslie, formed InfoLink Screening Services, Inc. together almost ten years ago after being married only four months. Actually it was Leslie's idea and she hired Barry. Between them they have three children and three grandchildren with plans for more grandchildren. On their day's off, they are avid horse people and trail ride and show.

Barry is a founding member and on the board of directors of the National Association of Professional Background Screeners (NAPBS) and the Association of Consumer Reporting Agencies (ACRA), and he is on the National Advisory Board of President & CEO Magazine.

As the established industry expert on the legal issues of employment background screening, he speaks nationally on the subject and has been a featured speaker at the national conventions for the Society for Human Resources Management (SHRM), National Human Resource Association (NHRA), Professionals in Human Resources Association (PIHRA), American Society for Industrial Security (ASIS), Association of Threat Assessment Professionals (ATAP), and many other organizations. Mr. Nadell has written articles for several magazines, has been featured on television including The Bloomberg Report and ABC News with Peter Jennings, and has been interviewed on more than one hundred live talk radio programs.

Mr. Nadell is a licensed private investigator under the Bureau of Security and Investigative Services in California (License No. PI 23882). He is not an attorney but is an associate member of the American, California State and Los Angeles Bar Associations specializing in labor and employment issues. He is a member of several human resources, management and security associations. In 2002, Mr. Nadell assisted the California Legislature in amending legislation and in 2004 he wrote and sponsored a bill to allow employers to provide reference information without fear of defamation lawsuits. He has testified in the California legislature on these and other bills important to human resource and security professionals. For more information, please call **(800) 990-4473 x1324** or visit **www.infolinkscreening.com**

Disclaimer

The enclosed information should not be construed as legal advice or legal opinion and is not necessarily complete. The material has been prepared by Barry J. Nadell for informational purposes only and is intended to provide a general overview of the topic of background screening. Before changing your current hiring practices, we strongly urge you seek qualified legal counsel admitted within your jurisdiction or in the jurisdictions you do business.

Introduction

The United States Department of Justice statistics for 2002 reveal that 6.7 million people—which translates to one in every 32 adults-are either jailed or in prison, or have been released on probation or parole. At least 95% of all state prison inmates will be released from prison at some point. About 80% are released under supervised parole. Recidivism is high; presently, 67.5% of all prisoners released are subsequently rearrested for a serious misdemeanor or felony within three years.

At the end of 2002, State and Federal prison authorities had under their jurisdiction 1,440,655 inmates; 1,277,127 of these were under State jurisdiction and 163,528 under Federal jurisdiction. Midyear 2002, local jails held or supervised 737,912 persons awaiting trial or serving a sentence. About 72,000 of these were persons serving their sentence in the community.

Unless you are diligent in performing background checks, some of these convicted criminals could wind up working for you, thus increasing the likelihood of violence in your workplace, theft of property, and legal action taken against you for negligent hiring liability.

Virtually every employer today is either considering doing background checks on potential employees or already performing them. Given the statistics on workplace violence, that's hardly surprising.

Workplace violence currently claims two million victims annually. *Homicide is one of the largest causes of workplace deaths for all employees and until 2002 was the single largest cause of workplace deaths for women employees today.* Not accidents, not medical conditions, but homicide. Almost a dozen people are murdered in the course of doing their jobs every week!

Homicide is obviously the most extreme form of workplace violence. However, we need to recognize that hostile behaviors such as yelling or screaming, threatening violence and fighting in the parking lot constitute workplace violence as well.

More than just recognizing this, we need to do everything in our power to prevent such behaviors from occurring.

It is important to note that a percentage of those who have been convicted of a crime do get rehabilitated and deserve a second chance working in society. Background screening is not simply to weed out anyone and everyone with a previous conviction from the workplace. It's purpose is to provide critical information to review to make an intelligent hiring decision. If you decide to do a background check, stick to information that is relevant to the job for which you are considering the applicant and verify all the information provided by that applicant.

Sleuthing 101

Background Checks and The Law

Background Checks Can Prevent Violence— And Protect Your Company As Well

The best way to prevent workplace violence is to perform careful, legally correct and extremely thorough background checks on all applicants for employment and eliminate any applicant who is not a good potential candidate for the particular position for which they are applying.

The second best way is to be alert to what's going on in your workplace and intervene before verbal violence becomes physical.

Almost every incidence of workplace violence is preceded by clear signals. An employee who exhibits angry, intimidating or aggressive behavior, has numerous conflicts with co-workers, seems fascinated by violence or shows desperation over personal problems is sending clear signals. Read and take them seriously!

A Few Examples of What Background Checks Revealed

It's amazing what you can learn from a background check. Here are a few examples:

Some time ago a woman applied to fill a job opening at InfoLink Screening Services, my national background screening company. InfoLink interviewers liked what they heard and asked the applicant to return on the following Monday for a second interview. On Friday InfoLink received her background check report, which revealed a current warrant for her arrest on drug charges.

The background check performed on another InfoLink job applicant revealed a burglary conviction which had occurred a year earlier. If this kind of thing can happen to a background screening company like InfoLink it can happen to every single one of you!

A background check InfoLink performed for another company revealed that the Social Security Number the applicant gave didn't belong to him. When confronted with this, the applicant had the gall to send us this e-mail: "How wonderful it is that we live in a country where people feel it's necessary to employ a digital Gestapo in order to weed out employees that don't happen to be the norm. This kind of thing always sets off alarms in my head, especially when the job is near minimum wage." He ranted on for another page and one-half.

A background check performed for a medical center uncovered the fact that the applicant was a convicted kidnapper-hardly the kind of person a medical center would want to hire!

A search done for another InfoLink client revealed that the applicant had been convicted of 22 felonies including five counts of burglary, five counts of credit card forgery, three counts of possession for sale and two counts of check forgery.

The subject of another background check had applied for a job at a home health agency. She was found to have been convicted of second-degree robbery. Three weeks after the background check, her name and picture appeared in the local paper because she was arrested for kidnapping and murdering a child.

Subjects of background checks have the right to dispute the information we find. One person who had been convicted of grand theft, burglary and credit card forgery with a current warrant for her arrest, disputed the information on her record. The following week the employer received an e-mail that purported to be from a judge in the court that verified the record. It read exactly as follows (removing the person's name of course): "Regarding case number . . . : The court, It cannot appreciate evidence to arrive at a conclusion in the matter, all charges have been dismissed. The charges were quashed. Case held for up to 6 months. I make this verification for (name) for and on behalf of the party for that reason. I am informed and believe, and on that ground allege, that the matters stated in it are true." Wow, you wonder what law school that judge graduated from! The employer sent the e-mail to us. We then sent it to the court, which issued an indictment on the charge of impersonating a court officer.

After reporting a conviction, one applicant asked that InfoLink amend our report because (in the attorney's words in his letter to InfoLink on October 23, 2003) "Anthony has completed his counseling and the case is *scheduled* to be dismissed on February 3, 2004." InfoLink advised that it would be pleased to do so after the February 3rd date once the court records showed the case was dismissed.

One InfoLink client, a major hotel chain, acquired several additional hotels and decided to do background checks on the employees of the hotels being purchased prior to hiring them. We found that one of the employees had been arrested on two counts of murder, two counts of armed robbery and one count of attempted murder. Because she was "not guilty by reason of insanity", these crimes were not reportable; however, her record also included some previous minor convictions that were reportable. As she still had the keys to the rooms in the hotel, this is a perfect example of why a hotel, or in fact any employer, needs to perform background checks!

A Cautionary Word About Temporary Employees

Few temporary agencies perform thorough background checks. One study InfoLink performed revealed that people who apply through a temporary agency have a criminal hit ratio approximately 70% greater than those who apply directly to the same company. One easy way to lower your odds of workplace violence and avoid bad hires is to make sure your temporary agency does background checks.

A temporary agency client of InfoLink requested a "hit ratio" report for the first six months of 2004. The report revealed that of the criminal searches performed, 23.5% included criminal convictions. Below is a list of some of the convictions found . . .

Assault with Firearm (F)
2 Counts of Arson (F)
2nd Degree Burglary (M)
Inflict Corporal Injury on Spouse (M)
Grand Theft Auto (M)
Petty Theft (M)
Assault & Battery (M)
Terrorist Threats (M)
Assault with a Deadly Weapon (M)
Receiving Stolen Property (F)
Possession of Drugs for Sale (F)
Forgery (F)
Burglery 1st Degree (F)—Probabition Violation—Sentenced to 2 yrs prison

One company that insisted its temporary agency perform background checks discovered that the agency had placed a convicted felon. When confronted with the fact that the screening company had provided this information, a representative of the temporary agency said, "You told us to run the background checks. You didn't tell us to look at them."

Theories of Negligent Hiring and Retention Liability

Courts have upheld theories of negligent hiring and negligent retention liability. "Negligent hiring occurs when, prior to the time the employee is actually hired, the employer knew or should have known of the employee's unfitness, and the issue of liability focuses upon the adequacy of the employer's pre-employment investigation into the employee's background." (Garcia v Duffy, 492 So. 2d 435 (1986)). Employers who fail to control or remove abusive, belligerent, or combative employees have been sued for the negligent hiring or negligent retention of employees who caused injury.

Typically, these suits have alleged that the employer failed to check references, criminal records, or general background information that would have shown the employee's propensity for criminal or tortuous behavior.

Employers have also been sued because they failed to dismiss or reassign an employee known to be potentially violent or abusive. This cause of action arises from the premise that an employer's prior knowledge of an employee's propensity for violence or other undesirable behaviors renders the employer liable for the results of that employee's behavior.

Some examples of this type of lawsuit are:

The Texas Supreme Court found in favor of a woman who alleged that a door-to-door salesman for the Kirby Vacuum Cleaner Company had raped her. The company had failed to perform a background check, which would have revealed previous complaints of sexual misconduct. "I hope this decision will cause Kirby to change it's ways to make sure that criminals are not sent into people's homes to sell Kirby vacuum cleaners," the rape victim said in a statement. "I also hope that it will prevent another woman from having to go through what my family and I have been through."

Justice Raul Gonzalez said Kirby's way of doing business—selling its products in customer's homes—poses a potential danger. "Kirby dealers, required to do in-home demonstrations, gain access to homes by virtue of the Kirby name. A person of ordinary intelligence should anticipate that an unsuitable dealer would pose a risk of harm," he wrote. The Texas Supreme Court upheld $160,000 in actual damages which was awarded to the plaintiff by a lower court but refused to support $800,000 in punitive damages levied against Kirby. *(Courtesy: Associated Press 01/02/99)*

In a California case, a fellow employee pushed an assistant sales manager at an auto dealership during an argument. The plaintiff sued his co-worker alleging assault and battery, and sued the dealership alleging "ratification" or the employer's "stamp of approval" on defendant employee's conduct.

An expert witness for the plaintiff testified that the push caused a permanent back injury. The plaintiff's attorney argued that defendant employer failed to discipline the co-worker and falsified witness statements.

Attorneys for the defendant employee and employer argued that the plaintiff started the scuffle and suffered from a pre-existing back injury and presented evidence that the defendant employee had been disciplined.

The trial lasted eleven days. The jury awarded the plaintiff $750,000.00.

The plaintiff could have sued his co-worker for assault and battery as a "civil wrong" regardless of where the altercation occurred. He was allowed to sue his employer because the scuffle occurred on work premises and, when informed of the incident, the employer failed to take disciplinary action against the co-worker because he was a top moneymaker for the dealership. (The San Francisco Daily Journal)

In another situation, the plaintiff, an independent contractor for a vending machine company sued the company for sexual harassment under Title VII of the 1964 Civil Rights Act. The Company argued that the plaintiff was not protected under Title VII as an employee because she worked under a signed agreement that specifically stated that she was an "independent sales representative."

The U.S. District Court for the Southern District of Texas examined the extent to which the Company controlled the work performed by its sales representatives and found that the employer exercised "considerable control" over the plaintiff's daily routine, sales techniques, and the manner in which her orders were processed.

The Court ruled that the plaintiff was an "employee" of the Company and allowed to proceed with her sexual harassment claim under Title VII. (EEOC v. Fawn Vendors, Inc., U.S. District Court, Southern District of Texas)

In February 2004, the Mesa, Arizona police asked the county attorney's office to charge a former volunteer girls' high school volleyball coach with two counts of sexual conduct with a minor. Meanwhile school officials were shocked because a criminal background check using fingerprinting by the Department of Public Safety did not alert them to the man's history of misdemeanors, including aggravated assault.

An employee of a Florida carpet cleaning franchise murdered several college students following a dispute with them over the employee's refusal to move furniture before cleaning their carpet.

The students' parents argued that the Florida franchise and the Texas-based franchiser should have been more diligent in checking the employee's background, which included dismissal by a former employer for carrying a concealed weapon and for violently resisting arrest for drug violations. The carpet franchise hired the employee one week after his arrest.

The carpet cleaning company argued that they had acted "reasonably" by contacting three of the employee's former employers. The employee informed his new company of his recent arrest and that the charges had been dismissed. The carpet company also argued that there was no evidence to indicate that the employee was prone to violence. He had apparently just "flipped out" on the day of the murders.

The jury found both franchise and franchiser liable for the negligent hiring and awarded the parents of the slain students one million dollars. (McKishnie v. Rainbow International Carpet Dying and Cleaning Co., Florida. March 1994)

In the largest negligent hiring case on record, the estate of a 32-year-old quadriplegic man murdered by his home health aide settled a lawsuit against the Visiting Nurse Association of Boston (VNA) and its agent, Trusted Health Resources, Inc., for negligently failing to conduct a background check on the aide, who had an extensive criminal record.

According to the complaint, after the aide assigned to John Ward failed to report to work a few times, Ward requested a replacement. Several weeks later, the aide returned to Ward's home and murdered him and his grandmother. This aide, who had been hired despite his failure to answer a question about prior criminal offenses, subsequently pleaded guilty to second-degree murder.

The suit alleged a simple phone call would have revealed the aide had lied about his qualifications. An expert for the estate testified at trial that criminal background checks have been standard practice since the mid-1980s for companies such as utilities and parcel delivery services that provide in-home services. A more in-depth reference check is required for home health aides than for employees providing other in-home services, the expert told the jury, because the home health care industry services a vulnerable population.

The VNA argued that although the aide had a theft record, it was unforeseeable he would commit murder. According to the estate's counsel, however, the VNA's failure to require criminal background checks made it foreseeable that any type of criminal could become a home health aide. Counsel said: "I was able to get even [defendants'] own hiring expert to admit on cross-examination that criminal background checks would have been a good practice."

The jury's award of $26.5 million included punitive damages. The estate's counsel hopes the verdict will serve to warn employers who serve vulnerable people in their homes that they must make reasonable efforts to adequately screen prospective employees. (Ward v. Trusted Health, No. 94-4297 Suffolk Super. Ct. 1991)

In June 2001, plaintiff Brian C., 15, was unlawfully imprisoned and sexually assaulted by a Los Angeles County Metro Transportation Authority bus driver while riding an LACMTA bus in Hollywood. Brian surreptitiously captured the audio portion of the assault on his camcorder. The bus driver was ultimately convicted of the crime and sentenced to 17 years in prison.

Brian sued the LACMTA, contending that it was liable for the bus driver's sexual assault of a passenger. He contended that the LACMTA was negligent in employing and supervising the bus driver, particularly because he had a prior felony conviction for a violent crime at the time he was hired. The case was settled in mediation for $1.85 million which the LACMTA will pay. (Brain C. v. Los Angeles County Metro Transportation Authority, No. BC277347 Los Angeles Superior Court 3/19/2004)

In another California case, a 27-year-old high school coach was accused of having unlawful sex with a minor. The plaintiff sued the school, alleging negligent hiring as the coach was hired without the school performing a criminal background check, which would have revealed a felony conviction and other drug convictions. The plaintiff settled the claim for $700,000 after mediation. (Jane Doe v. Unnamed School and John Roe, No. Confidential 3/5/2004)

If you are sued for negligent hiring liability, the first question your attorney will probably ask is "Did you do a background check?" If your answer is "No," and a subsequent investigation reveals an employee's prior criminal behavior, your attorney will most likely advise that you settle the case rather than go before a jury.

Falsified Employment Applications and Identification

Various studies have revealed that twenty to thirty percent of job applications contain false information. A study performed by the Society for Human Resource Management found that fifty three percent of the study sample had given false information about length of employment, fifty one percent about past salaries and forty five percent *falsely said they had no criminal records.*

Getting falsified identification is amazingly easy. When I was in New York recently a person on the street gave me a flyer that advertised instant identification cards.

I decided to check this out, and a few minutes later found myself in a dusty, rather seedy office on the Avenue of the Americas. People were lined up outside the door waiting to get in. When I got inside, I said to the person inside: "I got this flyer. What is this about?" He answered, "Well, we make I.D. cards" and I asked, "Really, I live in California. Can you make an I.D. card for me?" "No problem," the man replied.

When I said that I didn't have time to complete the form he told me I could mail it to him. So I sent in an application that contained completely false information except for my name and my picture. Three weeks later I received several different types of identification cards with my picture and a birth date making me fifteen years younger!

As a side note, after full disclosure and authorization has been received to perform background checks, of all criminal county searches performed by InfoLink in 2003, 8% revealed criminal convictions. In 2004, the overall hit ratio for criminal convictions increased to 8.4%. This figure differed by industry with the Auto Industry at 12.1%, Construction at 8.1%, Finance at 6.0%, Food Services at 12.4%, Healthcare at 5.7%, Hospitality at 8.6%, Manufacturing at 9.8%, Real Estate at 9.6%, Retail at 11.7%, Staffing at 8.5%, and Transportation at 10.7%. Searches in other categories in 2004 revealed hit ratios for DMV searches at 40.2%, Drug Testing at 3.3%, Credit History at 36%, Past Employment Referencing at 25.8%, Social Security Trace Verificationsat 4.2%, and Workers' Compensation at 8.3%. Hits may include convictions, MVR violations and accidents, discrepancies in employment and education verifications, positive drug tests, derogatory credit information, and workers' compensation claims.

Employee Theft and Lawsuits

Employee theft is a $400 billion industry, reported to take 6% of overall revenue. The recidivism rate for criminals today is reported to be 67.5%, so the odds are that convicted thieves will steal again when the opportunity presents itself. Don't give them that opportunity at your company.

In California, the jury awards to plaintiffs in employment law proceedings have ranged from $400,000 to $2.5 million during the past ten years. Only approximately fifty percent of the employers sued won their cases. Even those who won had the unfortunate experience of spending many hours and expensive legal fees, which are rarely recoverable. Legal fees, depending on the complexity of the issues, can be easily $100,000 or more.

Those are terrible odds! If you don't want to be sued, take extreme care when hiring.

The Wall Street Journal reported that a Dallas printing company sued an employment agency for placing an employee who embezzled $147,000. Both companies' names appeared in the article-hardly the kind of publicity either company wanted.

Plaintiffs' attorneys' ads in USA Today along with other publications suggest that if you're working, you can sue your employer. Suing employers beats ambulance chasing today.

Background Checks Reduce Turnover Costs

Employers performing background checks report that background checks reduce turnover. For more than 65 years William Mercer & Company has provided human resource solutions to companies in over 150 cities and 40 countries. A Mercer study found that in most cases turnover costs the company about $10,000 per job opening and costs can be as high as $30,000.

More specific studies break down the approximate employer cost as:
- Departing Employee: Productivity drops equal to one full month of the employee's last three months

- Vacant Position: On average, a position will remain empty for 13 weeks
- New Hire: New hires don't reach 100% efficiency for 11+ months
- Training: Managers spend an average of 14% of their time at work training new hires; co-workers of new hires spend 8% of their work time answering questions.

Good hiring involves much more than just finding the right people. It also requires training and paying the new hires before they become productive.

Our clients have told us that since they began obtaining thorough background checks their turnover costs have dropped sharply. One company realized enough savings to pay for a drug-testing program, which in turn further reduced the company's costs.

The Federal Fair Credit Reporting Act

In addition to protecting your employees from violence, you must also protect your company from engaging in unlawful background check practices. Therefore, you must understand the laws that govern the information that can be used for background checks and the methods of obtaining such information.

The most important law affecting background checks is the federal Fair Credit Reporting Act (FCRA), found in 15 U.S.C. § 1681 et seq.

The FCRA has been amended three times in the past seven years. The first amendment, which became effective on September 30, 1997, was the Consumer Credit Reporting Agencies Act. On December 4, 1998, the Clarification Act became effective. Finally, in 2004, we have the Fair and Accurate Credit Transactions Act (FACT Act). All three amendments shape the FCRA into what it is today.

It is critical to know that the FCRA has teeth. Before you can perform any background checks for employment using any third party, (i.e. a credit bureau, private investigator, record search firm, or consumer reporting agency), you must, by federal law, certify in writing to that agency that you understand the FCRA and will comply with it. Typically, when you open an account to perform background checks the consumer reporting agency will have such a section within their Agreement. Be very wary of any company that advertises it can perform background checks without a written agreement.

Performing background checks without an agreement that contains a certification violates federal law. The FCRA clearly says that a consumer reporting agency may furnish a consumer report for employment purposes *only if the person who receives the report from the agency certifies compliance with FCRA disclosure rules and will comply with FCRA adverse action rules if adverse action becomes applicable, and that information from the consumer report will not be used in violation of any equal employment opportunity law or regulation.*

Penalties for non-compliance include actual damages, punitive damages, costs and attorney's fees. Even worse, civil or criminal penalties may apply. Plaintiffs' attorneys know they can sue those who don't comply with the Fair Credit Reporting Act and at least recover attorney's costs if they prevail.

The FCRA pertains to all forms of background screening not just credit reports. Although it is the law anyone must comply with when performing background checks, §624 provides for any state laws which may be more restrictive. For example, the FCRA allows consumer reporting agencies to report criminal convictions as far back as the conviction occurred; however twelve states, listed on page 22, limit such reporting to seven years from the date of the conviction, parole, or release from prison.

To understand the FCRA, it is best to first review the definitions within the Act found in § 603. [15 U.S.C. § 1681a]

"Person" means any individual, partnership, corporation, trust, estate, cooperative, association, government or governmental subdivision or agency, or other entity.

"Consumer" means an individual.

"Consumer report" means any written, oral, or other communication of any information by a consumer reporting agency bearing on a consumer's credit worthiness, credit standing, credit capacity, character, general reputation, personal characteristics, or mode of living which is used or expected to be used or collected in whole or in part for the purpose of serving as a factor in establishing the consumer's eligibility for credit or insurance to be used primarily for personal, family, or household purposes; employment purposes; or any other purpose authorized under §604 [§ 1681b].

A consumer report does not include any report containing information solely as to transactions or experiences between the consumer and the person making the report; communication of that information among persons related by common ownership or affiliated by corporate control; or communication of other information among persons related by common ownership or affiliated by corporate control, if it is clearly and conspicuously disclosed to the consumer that the information may be communicated among such persons and the consumer is given the opportunity, before the time that the information is initially communicated, to direct that such information not be communicated among such persons; any authorization or approval of a specific extension of credit directly or indirectly by the issuer of a credit card or similar device; any report in which a person who has been requested by a third party to make a specific extension of credit directly or indirectly to a consumer conveys his or her decision with respect to such request, if the third party advises the consumer of the name and address of the person to whom the request was made, and such person makes the disclosures to the consumer required under section 615 [§ 1681m]; or a communication described in subsection (o) or (x) of §603. Subsection (o) refers to Investigative Consumer Reports and subsection (x) refers generally to consumer reports used for investigation of wrongdoing or violation of company policies.

Virtually anything you receive from a consumer reporting agency is a consumer report.

"Investigative consumer report" means a consumer report or portion thereof in which information on a consumer's character, general reputation, personal characteristics, or mode of living is obtained through personal interviews with neighbors, friends, or associates of the consumer reported on or with others with whom he is acquainted or who may have knowledge concerning any such items of information. However, such information shall not include specific factual information on a consumer's credit record obtained directly from a creditor of the consumer or from a consumer reporting agency when such information was obtained directly from a creditor of the consumer or from the consumer.

An example of an investigative consumer report is a past employment reference wherein you ask questions whereby the source provides opinions like: "how did they perform on their job", "would you rehire them", "how did they work with supervisors", or "did they exemplify management capabilities".

"**Consumer reporting agency**" ("CRA") means any person which, for monetary fees, dues, or on a cooperative nonprofit basis, regularly engages in whole or in part in the practice of assembling or evaluating consumer credit information or other information on consumers for the purpose of furnishing consumer reports to third parties, and which uses any means or facility of interstate commerce for the purpose of preparing or furnishing consumer reports.

CRA's include licensed private investigators and companies calling themselves record search firms. Thus any firm that provides a report for money is a CRA with exception to the federal government when background screening is performed via fingerprinting.

"**Employment purposes**" when used in connection with a consumer report means a report used for the purpose of evaluating a consumer for employment, promotion, reassignment or retention as an employee.

Thus the same rules apply whether background screening a job applicant or current employee except where the investigation is for wrongdoing or violating company policies.

"**Adverse action**" means a denial or cancellation of, an increase in any charge for, or a reduction or other adverse or unfavorable change in the terms of coverage or amount of, any insurance, existing or applied for, in connection with the underwriting of insurance; a denial of employment or any other decision for employment purposes that adversely affects any current or prospective employee; a denial or cancellation of, an increase in any charge for, or any other adverse or unfavorable change in the terms of, any license or benefit described in §604(a)(3)(D) [§ 1681b]; and an action taken or determination that is made in connection with an application that was made by, or a transaction that was initiated by, any consumer, or in connection with a review of an account under §604(a)(3)(F)(ii) [§ 1681b]; and adverse to the interests of the consumer.

Examples include not hiring, rescinding an offer, or firing a current employee.

FCRA Rules to Follow

Once one understands the definitions, a review of the provisions to follow is in order:

Two of the main provisions of the FCRA are DISCLOSURE and ADVERSE ACTION. These rules may not be altered by any state law. These provisions however, have been amended by the Fair and Accurate Credit Transactions Act of 2003 (the FACTAct) which offers employers some relief under certain conditions (see section on Workplace Investigations).

Section 604(b)(2) of the FCRA, in general states that a person may not procure a consumer report, or cause a consumer report to be procured, for employment purposes with respect to any consumer, unless a clear and conspicuous disclosure has been made in writing to the consumer at any time before the report is procured or caused to be procured, in a document that consists solely of the disclosure, that a consumer report may be obtained for employment purposes; and the consumer has authorized in writing. Such authorization may be made on the same disclosure document. Therefore, when outsourcing background screening, the employer must use a separate document from the employment application as disclosure. (See FTC Staff Opinion Letter of December 18, 1997, to Harold R. Hawkey).

Further, when requesting an investigative consumer report on any consumer, the disclosure must clearly and accurately disclose to the consumer that an investigative consumer report including information as to their character, general reputation, personal characteristics and mode of living, whichever are applicable, may be made. The disclosure must be made in writing mailed, or otherwise delivered, to the consumer, not later than three days after the date on which the report was first requested. It also must include a statement informing the consumer of his right to request the additional disclosures including the nature and scope of investigation and a written summary of their rights prepared pursuant to section 609(c) [§ 1681g].

In general, in using a consumer report for employment purposes, before taking any adverse action based in whole or in part on the report, the person intending to take such adverse action shall provide to the consumer to whom the report relates a copy of the report; and a description in writing of the rights of the consumer, as prescribed by the Federal Trade Commission under §609(c)(3). (Commonly known as the "FTC Rights Document").

The third provision of the FCRA relates to the use of the information itself. Please review the laws within your state for more restrictive requirements. §605 [15 U.S.C. §1681c] lists information that must be excluded from consumer reports. These include:

1. Cases under Title 11 [United States Code] or under the Bankruptcy Act that, from the date of entry of the order for relief or the date of adjudication, as the case may be, antedate the report by more than 10 years.
2. Civil suits, civil judgments, and records of arrest that from date of entry, antedate the report by more than seven years or until the governing statute of limitations has expired, whichever is the longer period.
3. Paid tax liens which, from date of payment, antedate the report by more than seven years.
4. Accounts placed for collection or charged to profit and loss which antedates the report by more than seven years.
5. Any other adverse item of information, other than records of convictions of crimes which antedates the report by more than seven years.

These exclusions are not applicable in the case of any consumer credit report to be used in connection with:

1. A credit transaction involving, or which may reasonably be expected to involve, a principal amount of $150,000 or more;
2. The underwriting of life insurance involving, or which may reasonably be expected to involve, a face amount of $150,000 or more; or

3. The employment of any individual at an annual salary which equals, or which may reasonably be expected to equal $75,000, or more.

Legally Permissible Purposes for Background Checks

Some companies advertise they can get you any information you want on anyone. It is important to note that consumers have privacy rights and the FCRA prohibits delving into someone's background without a permissible purpose.

Permissible purposes include:

(1) In response to the order of a court having jurisdiction to issue such an order, or a subpoena issued in connection with proceedings before a Federal grand jury
(2) In accordance with the written instructions of the consumer to whom it relates
(3) For a credit transaction involving the consumer on whom the information is to be furnished and to whom credit may be extended
(4) To review or collect a consumer account
(5) For employment purposes
(6) For insurance underwriting that involves the consumer
(7) To determine the consumer's eligibility for a license or other benefit that requires considering an applicant's financial responsibility or status
(8) To evaluate or assess the credit or prepayment risks associated with an existing credit obligation by a potential investor or servicer or current insurer
(9) For a legitimate business need such as a transaction initiated by the consumer or to review an account to determine whether the consumer is meeting the terms of the account as agreed
(10) In response to a request by the head of a state or local child support enforcement agency or a state or its authorized representative with certification that the consumer report is needed to establish ability to pay child support or determine the level of child support payments and that the consumer was provided with at least 10 days' prior notice to the consumer that the report will be requested, kept confidential, used solely for a purpose described and for no other purpose
(11) In response to a request from agency administering a state plan under Section 454 of the Social Security Act (42 U.S.C. § 654) for use to set an initial or modified child support award

"Legitimate business need" may sound like a caveat that allows searching for any reason, but it's not. A legitimate business need means a business transaction initiated by the consumer or to review an existing account to confirm that the terms agreed to are met.

When you offer credit to a potential client you may perform a background check. Unless you hired a licensed private investigator, you may not do a background check on your daughter's boyfriend unless he has given written permission to do so. The same issue would exist if you wanted a background check on a friend or neighbor. Remember, privacy is an important right and you must be careful not to violate someone's privacy.

Some companies use contractors or volunteers. Contractors and volunteers are not employees. *If your company uses independent contractors or volunteers and you want to do background checks, make sure that your form specifically asks for their written permission and is correctly worded so that you have legal authority to obtain a background report.*

Today, more and more companies do background checks on independent contractors and other non-employees who come on to their sites. A few years ago InfoLink developed a program called "vendor on premises" that as a condition of doing business with the company requires vendors to do background checks on their people at their cost before sending a person. This program is especially important in states where the employer is legally liable for the acts of vendors and independent contractors.

The Federal Trade Commission

The Federal Trade Commission (FTC) is the watchdog of the Fair Credit Reporting Act, and issued staff opinion letters on various subjects. FTC staff opinion letters are not law; they are just opinions, although no one as yet has challenged these opinions in court. We recommend that if they issued an opinion, you need to follow it. You may find all the FTC Staff Opinion letters at www.ftc.gov.

My first question to the FTC was, "If you do fingerprinting does that make the federal government a consumer-reporting agency?" *The answer was no, the consumer-reporting rules don't apply if you fingerprint, though I don't know why they shouldn't.*

The most important FTC staff opinion letters relating to background screening are:

- HUXWELL (Disclosures may not contain a "waiver" of the consumer's rights but may include identifying information)
- NADELL (Reporting Adverse Information—7 yr. limit waived for reporting negative information found in references and education verifications)
- ALLAN (Stored Data Public Records are generally not accurate indicating employers should use caution and follow § 606 (d)(3) [15 U.S.C. § 1681d] and § 613 (1) [15 U.S.C. § 1681k] regarding reporting of database information)
- ALLAN (Adverse Action Notice required and is the employer's responsibility)
- WILLNER (Investigative Consumer Reports-within 3 days, send consumer the FTC rights notice)
- JAMES (With proper wording, Disclosures may only need be authorized once)
- LEATHERS (A disclosure may not be part of an employment application)
- HOLLAND (Reporting of Warrants-no time limit)
- SLYTER/LEBLANC (Private Investigators and "record search firms" are Consumer Reporting Agencies if they charge for their services)

Steps to Take Prior to Performing a Background Check

Proper Disclosure

The first and most important step in complying with the FCRA is disclosing to the consumer that you may be requesting a background search (consumer report) from a consumer-reporting agency. The disclosure must be clear, conspicuous, and made in writing in a stand-alone document to the consumer at any time before the report is procured. The consumer must authorize the disclosure in writing and may do so on the disclosure document.

Why the word "may"? Most companies perform background checks only on the final candidates for employment, although they offer disclosure forms to all candidates who apply. Legislators were wise to use the word "may" as opposed to "will" for this reason.

Chances are no company will be sued if your form says that you "will" do a background check, but change "will" to "may" to be legal.

Job applicants for employment who apply by mail, telephone or computer must also receive notice that the employer may obtain a consumer-report and must give oral, written or electronic consent before the report is procured.

One exception to "written" authorization applies to positions over which the Secretary of Transportation has power to establish qualifications and maximum hours of service or to a position subject to safety regulation by a State transportation agency when the employment application was submitted by mail, telephone, computer, or other similar means.

Note that the transportation industry has special rules. Truckers may consent to a background check orally because they may not be able to easily consent in writing. Further, adverse action normally needs to be in writing but in the trucking industry it can be oral as well.

California is the most restrictive state regarding background screening laws. California adds requirements which we believe do not place undue burdens or liability on employers and may be extended to disclosure forms used in other states. This saves the trouble of having two separate disclosure forms or a California Addendum.

California requires that you (1) identify the Consumer Reporting Agency conducting the background check; (2) indicate that the check may bear on their character, reputation, personal characteristics, and mode of living; and (3) provide a summary of the consumers' rights under §1786.22 of the California Consumers Investigative Reporting Agencies Act.

§1786.22 requires that (1) you indicate on your disclosure form that the CRA shall supply files and information during normal business hours and on reasonable notice; (2) such files shall be available for visual inspection in person after supplying proper identification, or by certified mail after written request, or by telephone if a written request is made with proper identification; (3) a copy shall be available for a fee not to exceed the actual costs of duplication; (4) the CRA shall provide trained personnel to explain any information and shall provide a written explanation of any coded information contained in the file; (5) the consumer shall be permitted to be accompanied by one other person of their choosing who shall furnish reasonable identification. Finally, should a report be mailed to a consumer by the CRA, the CRA shall provide a written notice in simple plain English and Spanish setting forth the terms and conditions of their right to receive all disclosures.

Finally California (along with Minnesota and Oklahoma) requires that your disclosure form contain a box that the consumer may check should they wish a copy of the consumer report. These states' law includes this requirements for any investigative report or credit report.

More Than Half of Disclosure Forms Violate the Law

More than half of the disclosure forms seen by our office violate federal or state law or both.

The most flagrant violation of FCRA is a form which includes a waiver by the consumer of his or her rights. Including such a waiver in a disclosure form violates Section 604(b)(2)(A) of the FCRA, which requires that a disclosure consist "solely" of the disclosure that a consumer report may be obtained for employment purposes. Moreover, it is a general principle of law that benefits provided to citizens by federal statute generally may not be waived by private agreement unless Congress intended such a result. *Brooklyn Savings Bank v. O'Neill*, 324 U.S. 697 (1945). The FCRA does not authorize any waiver of rights, nor does the legislative history show that Congress intended that consumers should be able to sign away their legal rights under the Act. (See: FTC Opinion Letter with Hauxwell of 6-12-1998)

Disclosure forms are generally provided by background screening companies. Employers should carefully review all forms provided to them and refuse to retain a background screening company that offers forms that violate the law.

Some examples of language that violates the FCRA are:

"I release (company name) and or its agents and any person that provides or uses information pursuant to this authorization from any and all liability claims or lawsuits in relation to the information obtained from any and all of the above referenced sources."

"I voluntarily, knowingly and unconditionally release any person from any and all liability."

"I agree to release and hold harmless the background screening company from any liabilities arising from errors in information it provides." (Why would you hire this

15

background screening company? They are telling you they are going to make errors right up front!)

"I waive any right that I may have to inspect information"

"XYZ Background Screening Company shall not be liable for the information within its reports as it must rely on accuracy from 'public record data sources' which is infallible"

"Information is accepted by you without any liability on the part of the background screening company"

In addition, according to guidelines from the U.S. Equal Employment Opportunity Commission (EEOC) disclosure forms may not ask for gender, race, or maiden name; and be cautious asking for the applicant's full date of birth. These questions must be left (if asked at all) until an employer actually offers employment or a conditional job offer.

The EEOC website at: **http://www.eeoc.gov/facts/age.html** provides The Age Discrimination Employment Act of 1967 (ADEA) which does not specifically prohibit an employer from asking an applicant's age or date of birth. However, because such inquiries may defer older workers from applying for employment or may otherwise indicate possible intent to discriminate based on age, requests for age information will be closely scrutinized to make sure that the inquiry was made for a lawful purpose, rather than for a purpose prohibited by the ADEA. ADEA protects individuals who are 40 years of age or older from employment discrimination based on age. The ADEA's protections apply to both employees and job applicants. Under the ADEA, it is unlawful to discriminate against a person because of his/her age with respect to any term, condition, or privilege of employment—including, but not limited to, hiring, firing, promotion, layoff, compensation, benefits, job assignments, and training. The ADEA applies to employers with 20 or more employees, including state and local governments. It also applies to employment agencies and to labor organizations, as well as the federal government.

The following is excerpted from EEOC Notice N-015.043 "Job Advertising and Pre-Employment Inquires Under the Age Discrimination in Employment Act (ADEA)", Section II. Pre-Employment Inquiries:

"The Commission has addressed the issue of pre-employment inquiries concerning age in two separate provisions.

The second provision, 20 C.F.R. §1625.5, focuses on requests for age on employment application forms. The Commission regulation at 29 C.F.R. §1625.5 provides in part: A request on the part of an employer for information such as "Date of Birth" or "State Age" on an application form is not, in itself, a violation of the Act. The purpose of section 1625.5 is to insure that older applicants are judged on ability rather than age. To assure applicants in the protected age group that an inquiry as to age is for a permissible purpose, employers should include a reference on the application form stating that the employer does not discriminate on the basis of age. Another option would be to explain to each applicant the specific reason why the information concerning age is being requested.

NOTE: In fiscal year 2002, the EEOC received 19,921 charges of age discrimination. EEOC resolved 18,673 age discrimination charges in FY 2002 and recovered $55.7 million in monetary benefits for charging parties and other aggrieved individuals (not including monetary benefits obtained through litigation). see: **http://www.eeoc.gov/typs/age.html**

As a national background screening company, InfoLink prefers to have the full date of birth in advance as the DOB is the primary identifier and almost always the only identifier in a criminal file. In addition, several states require the full DOB in order to obtain a motor vehicle report (not California). Finally some jurisdictions do not allow a criminal record search without the full date of birth in advance. Where a client is comfortable asking for full DOB, InfoLink offers a disclosure form that asks for it with a statement that it is for identifying purposes only.

Notwithstanding, most of InfoLink's clients prefer to be conservative and not invite a potential age discrimination issue by asking only for month and day of birth before making an offer of employment. InfoLink's normal disclosure form, and the one asked for most, requests only month and day of birth. In order to obtain the year of birth InfoLink obtains it from the applicant on behalf of the client by email, phone, or the applicant provides it by logging into a special secure website. By offering this service, companies have a comfort level.

The bottom line is that employers need to do what is comfortable, and if only asking for month and day before making an offer of employment is more comfortable, then you need to have your background screening company obtain the year directly from the applicant. Your legal counsel would be the best source to advise your further in this area.

An applicant who knows the law and refuses to sign an unlawful disclosure form and is refused employment; or, one who doesn't know the law and signs the unlawful form and whose background check reveals criminal activity, is a lawsuit waiting to happen.

Additional rules apply to investigative consumer reports. When an investigative consumer report is included in the background check, the disclosure form must reveal that that information will be collected which may bear on the applicant's "character, general reputation, personal characteristics and mode of living." It must also include a statement informing the consumer of his right to request the additional disclosures plus a written summary of the rights of the consumer prepared pursuant to section 609(c) [§ 1681g].

Employers may obtain a general or "blanket" authorization from the consumer to obtain consumer reports at any time during the consumer's tenure of employment. Make sure that your disclosure form states that permission to perform a background check is *both during the period of application and during the course of employment.* That way, if you're promoting an employee two years after the initial hire and want to do a new background check or investigation, the employee doesn't have to sign a new disclosure form. There may be a few states with issues and we recommend you obtain advice from legal counsel within your state. (See FTC Opinion "James" dated 8-5-1998). The James opinion specifically indicated that: "Section 604(b)(2) does not specifically address the issue of whether a disclosure must be made, and permission obtained, each time a consumer report is obtained. However, at each place where what is not Section 604(b)(2) is discussed in a number of Congressional committee reports that accompanied proposals to amend Section 604, Congress indicates that employers do not need to go through the disclosure/authorization process each time a report is requested; rather, Congress indicates that the employer may obtain a general or "blanket" authorization from the consumer to obtain consumer reports at any time during the consumer's tenure of employment."

Various states have expanded federal law and incorporated provisions to be included in disclosure forms that employers must review. California law is the most comprehensive. It includes provisions for:

(1) Identifying the consumer reporting agency performing the background check
(2) Indicating that the report may bear on the consumers character, general reputation, personal characteristics, or mode of living
(3) Including a summary of the consumers rights under California Civil Code section 1786.22; and
(4) California, Minnesota and Oklahoma require disclosure forms to have a box that applicants can check if they want to receive a copy of their background check report.

Use the Disclosure form to
Compare Background Screening Companies

When comparing one Consumer Reporting Agency (CRA) to another, be sure to review the disclosure forms they provide. A form that violates the FCRA is a red flag. If the CRA doesn't understand the laws that surround their industry, will the CRA's reports be accurate? Can you trust them to comply with other legal requirements? To the extent that you rely on the information and forms provided, will your business experience increased risk of lawsuits?

When analyzing disclosure forms offered by CRA's, look for these common mistakes that may make the forms unlawful:

1. Does the form indicate that a background check "will" be performed?
2. Does the form include a "waiver" of the consumer's rights or release the CRA from liability?
3. Does the form attempt to do tasks other than simply be a disclosure?
4. Does the form indicate the name of the consumer-reporting agency performing the search?
5. Does the form indicate that the information may bear on the person's character, general reputation, personal characteristics, or mode of living?
6. Does the form indicate that the consumer has the right to obtain additional infor-

mation as to the nature and scope of the search?

7. Does the form ask the consumer to provide sensitive information before receiving an offer of employment like, full date of birth, maiden name, sex, or race?
8. If the employer seeking reports is in California, Minnesota, or Oklahoma, does the disclosure form have a box that the consumer can check off to receive a copy of the report?
9. California law requires the disclosure to summarize the provisions of Section 1786.22 of the Civil Code. All five provisions must be included in a disclosure document in California. Does the CRA have a separate form as a "California Amendment" or does it incorporate these consumer rights for use nationwide. Our opinion is that these rights in California are reasonable and why not offer them nationwide?
10. Does the form contain language that allows the document be a "multi-use" form, enabling you to perform another background check in the future while the consumer is an employee with the company without obtaining a new signature?

Beware of Negligent Reporting Liability

Beware that the contract or agreement the CRA wants you to sign doesn't relieve the CRA of liability for negligent reporting. Never trust a consumer reporting agency that doesn't accept responsibility for its level of reporting. Accuracy is critical!
We have seen clauses in agreements such as:

"End User will indemnify, defend, and hold (background screening company) harmless from any and all liabilities, damages, losses, claims, costs and expenses, including reasonable attorneys fees, which may be asserted against or incurred by (background screening company) arising out of or resulting from the use, disclosure, sale, or transfer of the services (or information therein) by End User or its customers..." "End User covenants not to sue or maintain any cause of action, claim, demand, cross-claim, third party action or other form of litigation or arbitration against (background screening company), its officer's, directors, employees, contractors, agents, affiliated bureaus, or subscribers arising out of relating in any way to the Services (or information therein) being blocked by (background screening company) not being accurate, timely, complete or current."

Some waivers are not as blatant. Other agreements say: "The "Vendor" is not liable in any way for any loss or injury resulting from the furnishing of such information and does not guarantee its accuracy". Some CRA's have statements in very small print on their report. One indicated: "By engaging (background screening company), you release (the background screening company) and all of its officers, agents, and employees from all liability for any negligence associated with providing the enclosed information."

Workplace Investigations

In 1999, the Federal Trade Commission's staff published the notorious "Vail" letter that caused much consternation for employers seeking to comply with the FCRA during third-party investigations of workplace wrongdoing.

Such investigations included misconduct in discrimination or harassment, threat of violence, theft, embezzlement or other types of fraud against the employer or customers, and controlled substances. Confidential interviews, undercover investigators, or both best serve the employers in these settings.

Unfortunately, the FTC staff determined in a letter to Ms. Judi Vail (April 5, 1999) that sexual harassment investigations conducted by third-party investigators are likely to be considered "investigative consumer reports" covered by the FCRA's procedural requirement requiring disclosure and prior written authorization.

In response, HR 2622 "The Fair and Accurate Credit Transactions Act of 2003" (the FACT Act) which added procedures to protect consumers from identity theft, also amended the FCRA to exempt certain communications from the definition of consumer report. This exemption relieved employers from the onerous requirements of disclosure when hiring an outside third party to conduct investigations.

The FACT Act waives the disclosure requirement for investigations due to suspicion of misconduct relating to employment, for investigations required to comply with federal, state, or local laws and regulations, and for suspicion of violation of any preexisting written policies of the employer. *However, if an employer requires a credit investigation as part of the investigation a written disclosure and authorization is still required.*

Electronic Signatures

How does "disclosure forms authorized in writing" apply to the federal electronic signature act? The Electronic Signatures in Global and National Commerce Act (the ESIGN Act) found at Pub. L. No. 106-229, 114 Stat. 464 / 15 U.S.C. § 7001 *et seq.*, was signed into law on June 30, 2000, and became primarily effective on October 1, 2000, granting legal force to electronic signatures, contracts, and other records.

Section 101(a) of the ESIGN Act sets forth the following general rule:

(a) . . . Notwithstanding any statute, regulation, or other rule of law (other than this title and title II), with respect to any transaction in or affecting interstate or foreign commerce—(1) a signature, contract, or other record relating to such transaction may not be denied legal effect, validity, or enforceability solely because it is in electronic form.

According to the FTC "because Section 604(a)(2) of the FCRA requires 'written instructions', the consumer's electronic authorization is a 'record' that must be 'capable of being retained and accurately reproduced for later reference' for the benefit of the consumer. While a consumer's consent is not invalid merely because it is communicated in electronic form, that electronic authorization must be in a form that can be retained and retrieved in perceivable form, as specified by Section 101(e) of the ESIGN Act."

A word of caution: Electronic disclosure forms may become commonplace in the future, but referral sources and educational facilities now ask that consumer-reporting agencies to supply a "hand written signature" authorizing the agency to obtain personal verification information.

Adverse Action

Once again, adverse action is considered any negative action taken against a consumer which was based in whole or in part on the consumer report issued by the consumer reporting agency. These actions include: not hiring the person, firing them, or rescinding an offer or conditional offer.

Adverse action is a three-step process. First, you must give the applicant a copy of the report along with a copy of his or her rights as prescribed by the FTC. Then you must allow the applicant a reasonable period of time in which to dispute the information. Unfortunately there is NO legal definition of a "reasonable period of time". However, within the commentary behind the FCRA, the legislators seemed to indicate that five business days was reasonable.

Only after the reasonable period of time can you take adverse action, which must be in writing. There are two exceptions to adverse action rules (1) Within the Clarification Act signed December 4, 1998, for those who come under jurisdiction of the Department of Transportation wherein adverse action may be provided orally allowing for a "reasonable period of time" to dispute the information within the report specific to three days. (2) Within the FACTAct which somewhat alters adverse action due to an investigation which is the subject of this Act.

A good practice is, if a report contains anything negative at all, follow the adverse action rules and give the applicant the opportunity to dispute the information. Even the most obscure piece of negative information, even if not used in the hiring decision, might be grounds for a lawsuit if the applicant is denied a job without being offered the right to dispute the findings of the report.

In the United States of America, Plaintiff, v. Imperial Palace, Inc. two casinos denied consumers jobs based on their credit reports without following adverse action procedures and informing them of their rights under the FCRA. The complaint and consent decree was filed July 13, 2004 in U.S. District court-Nevada. The defendants agreed to pay $325,000 in civil penalties for their failure to provide the defendants with the required notices. (FTC File No. 0323050, Civ. No. CV-S-04-0963-RLH-PAL)

The Fair and Accurate Transactions Act of 2003 amended the FCRA for investigations conducted because of suspicion of wrongdoing, violating company policies or any other permissible purpose described in the Act. When taking Adverse Action due to such investigation based in whole or in part on the report, the employer shall disclose to the consumer a summary containing the nature and substance of the communication upon which the adverse action is based, except that the sources of information acquired solely for use in preparing an investigative consumer report need not be disclosed. In other words, the employer may remove the names of sources that relate to any interviews with persons required in the investigation but may not remove sources of items researched in a consumer report like criminal information, drivers' license information, or other such sources of factual data.

Time Frames for Criminal Reports

Before the federal Clarification Act, federal law indicated a CRA could only report criminal convictions for seven years from the date of conviction, parole or release from prison. The Clarification Act amended this section so that CRA may report criminal convictions regardless of how long ago the conviction occurred.

Unfortunately, state laws still apply. Twelve states limit the reporting of a conviction to seven years from the date of conviction, end of parole or release from prison. Of the twelve states, four allow reporting beyond seven years if the subject earns or is expected to earn a particular threshold amount. See chart below:

California	§1785.13.6 & §1786.18.7	7 years	
Colorado	CRS §12-14.3-105.3	7 years	$75K Income Exception
Kansas	§50-704	7 years	
Maryland	§14-1203	7 years	
Massachusetts	MGL §93-52	7 years	
Montana	MCA §31-3-112	7 years	
Nevada	NRS §598C.150	7 years	
New Hampshire	HRS §359-B:5	7 years	
New Mexico	§56-3-6	7 years	
New York	ART 25- §380-j	7 years	$25K Income Exception
Texas	CH 20 §20.05	7 years	$75K Income Exception
Washington	RWC 19.182.040	7 years	$20K Income Exception

What does "from the date of conviction, parole or release from prison" mean? It means that in June 2004, a consumer-reporting agency cannot report a conviction made in 1995; however, if the subject was released from prison in 2000, the crime may be reported because the release from prison occurred within seven years.

Employers who obtain information directly from the courts are not subject to a seven-year limitation except where state law prohibits such look back. For example, in

South Dakota employers may inquire only about felonies committed within the past seven years; Massachusetts allows only a seven-year review for felonies and five year review for most misdemeanors, excepting first offenses.

Accuracy of Reports

Section 606 (d)(3) [15 U.S.C. § 1681d] of the FCRA specifically indicates that except for § 613 of the FCRA (see below) a Consumer Reporting Agency may not disclose public records for arrest, indictment, conviction, civil judicial action, tax lien, or outstanding judgment, unless the agency has verified the accuracy of the information during the 30-day period ending on the date on which the report is furnished.

§ 613 (1) [15 U.S.C. § 1681k] indicates that when a consumer-reporting agency furnishes a consumer report for employment purposes that contains public records likely to have an adverse effect upon a consumer's ability to obtain employment, it must maintain strict procedures to insure that this information is complete and up to date. Public records for arrests, indictments, convictions, suits, tax liens, and outstanding judgments are considered up to date if the current public record status of the item at the time of the report is reported or the consumer is notified that public record information is being reported and given the name and address of the person seeking the information at the time of the report.

Although § 613 (1) seems to allow the reporting of inaccurate public record information, several states specifically require that prior to reporting information, the consumer reporting agency must verify its accuracy. State codes for these states in general state "Whenever a consumer reporting agency prepares a consumer report, the agency shall follow reasonable procedures to assure maximum possible accuracy of the information concerning the consumer about whom the report relates". These states are Arizona, California, Colorado, Kansas, Maine, Maryland, Massachusetts, Montana, New Hampshire, New Jersey, New York and Washington.

Due to the inaccuracies of databases, we strongly recommend that negative information from any database is verified through a county court records search.

It is important to note that a consumer reporting agency shall not prepare or furnish an investigative consumer report on a consumer that contains information that is adverse to the interest of the consumer and that is obtained through a personal interview with a neighbor, friend, or associate of the consumer or with another person with whom the consumer is acquainted or who has knowledge of such item of information, unless the agency has followed reasonable procedures to obtain confirmation of the information, from an additional source that has independent and direct knowledge of the information; or the person interviewed is the best possible source of the information.

Information That Is Available

Criminal history is the primary service requested in background screening. Consumer Reporting Agencies may report convictions, whether the subject is out on bail on their own recognizance pending trial, and current outstanding warrants.

Given that there are approximately 3,144 counties and over 5,000 repositories, the only way to get completely accurate information is to hire a nationwide company that can go to any court and research the physical records.

Felonies represent only about 27% of criminal filings. Approximately 2.5% of all criminal searches reported have a felony. It's critical to inquire and learn about an applicant's felony and misdemeanor conviction record. Only in South Dakota is an employer limited to asking only about felony convictions. Massachusetts limits asking about misdemeanors to those that are more than five years old and not a first offense and limits inquiring about felonies to the previous seven years. California and several other states consider assault, battery, sexual battery, theft and brandishing a weapon as misdemeanors.

Most databases contain only felony records and in some states fingerprint files reveal only felonies. On February 11, 2004, the Arizona Republic reported that the Mesa police arrested a former volunteer girls' high school volleyball coach with two counts of sexual conduct with a minor. To screen volunteers, the school had relied on fingerprints on file with the Department of Public Safety, which only took fingerprints of felons. School administrators were shocked to learn, after the subject had sexually assaulted a young girl, that he had eight misdemeanors on his record.

Studies performed by consumer reporting agencies reveal that database searches for multiple counties or searches purported to be "national" consistently miss both felony and serious misdemeanor convictions and may report cases that were actually expunged or dismissed.

Review your employment application. Often an employer asks only about felonies, hires the subject and later learns that they were convicted of serious misdemeanors. Because the individual didn't falsify their application, the employer has no grounds to rescind the offer of employment based on falsifying their application.

In some states the district attorney decides whether to prosecute for a felony or a misdemeanor. Arrests for embezzlement may be decided on how much money was embezzled. Should an employer care? I don't know any employer who would hire an applicant who embezzled no matter the amount when the applicant was applying for a position which could affect the company financially!

On a final note, we often see that a person was charged with several crimes but because of plea-bargaining was convicted only of a misdemeanor offense. Employers must be careful—where there is smoke, fire usually precipitates.

Court Records

Note: When researching court records, dismissed cases are somewhat akin to forgiveness. Expunging a record wipes the record clean as if the crime had never occurred.

County court records are found within the Municipal or Superior records of the particular county. Generally, Superior Court crimes are felonies only; however, some states have merged records. Almost any time an arrest and conviction is made by local authorities, the records will be found in the County court.

Federal Criminal Cases

Federal criminal cases do not appear in local court records, so be sure the CRA you hire checks the applicable Federal District Court records. Search of U.S. Federal districts provides convictions of crimes that occurred on federal property and convictions of federal laws such as tax evasion, mail and wire fraud, drug trafficking, immigration law violations and postal offenses. Records provide a criminal history from the date of disposition, parole or release from imprisonment. A better search is to request a National Federal District Court Search which is a nationwide search covering *all* U.S. Federal districts excluding Alaska, Guam, Idaho, new Mexico and Northern Marina Islands.

When performing a background search for a well known entertainment company located in Los Angeles, California; a search for criminal convictions in all counties of previous residence, a search of the state's sexual offender database listing, and also a search of the national criminal database; all sources reported the subject "clear". However, when searching the federal district courts nationally, the subject was found to have been convicted for mail fraud, bank fraud, and money laundering in Oklahoma in 1996 and imprisoned for 51 months. Both her credit report and social security trace report confirmed that she had lived in Oklahoma in 1996.

State Incarceration Records

State incarceration records tell when someone was incarcerated in state prison and the date of release. State and federal district prison records are updated 48 hours after inmates are paroled. The search reveals if the subject has served time in prison for a felony conviction, providing their release date, any current warrant information for parole violations, and sometimes a picture I.D. This statewide search may be conducted in addition to county criminal searches for greater due diligence where statewide information is not available from a state repository.

Once, InfoLink found that an applicant had been convicted of two counts of murder, one count of attempted murder, and one count of carrying an assault weapon and had been sentenced to 37 years in state prison. The applicant's first name, middle initial and last name matched, date of birth, Social Security Number and drivers' license numbers also all matched; but, something seemed wrong. When we searched the state incarceration records we found that the person matched was still in jail. It was apparent that the applicant had bought a phony identification. His own ID couldn't have been worse!

Such incarceration records often don't reveal the crime or case number only if the individual was incarcerated and released with the date of release. For case information, a national criminal search or a search of the state repository (if available) would provide the jurisdiction to research the case for accuracy.

State Repository Records Are Often Out of Date

Some states maintain record repositories, database records compiled from information sent by county courts to the state. Often, by the time the state sells the information it's old and may be inaccurate. Repository records must be confirmed by hand searches at the county level.

State Repository searches are not available in all states. The chart below contains only those states in which Repository Searches are available. Note, access fees may change without notice.

State	Requirements	CRA Must Have Disclosure Faxed	Expected Turnaround Time (Not Guaranteed)	Access Fees
Alabama	Full DOB/SSN	No	3 days	$6.00
Arkansas	Full DOB/SSN	Yes	3 days	$12.00
Colorado	Full DOB/SSN	Yes	3 days	$5.50
Connecticut	Full DOB/SSN	Yes	3 days	$7.00
Delaware	Full DOB/SSN	Yes	3 days	$9.00
Florida	Full DOB/SSN	Yes	3 days	$23.00
Georgia	Full DOB/SSN	Yes	3 days	$6.00
Hawaii	Full DOB/SSN	No	3 days	$10.00
Idaho	Full DOB/SSN	Yes	3 days	$15.00
Illinois	Full DOB/SSN	No	10–15 days	$7.00
Indiana	Full DOB/SSN	Yes	3 days	$13.00
Iowa	Full DOB/SSN	Yes	3 days	$20.00
Kansas	Full DOB/SSN	Yes	1–3 weeks	$15.00
Kentucky	Full DOB/SSN	Yes	3 days	$18.00
Maryland	Full DOB/SSN	Yes	4 days	$13.00
Michigan	Full DOB/SSN	Yes	3 days	$15.00
Minnesota	Full DOB/SSN	Yes	3 days	$8.00
Mississippi	Full DOB/SSN	No	3 days	$13.00

Missouri	Full DOB/SSN	Yes	3 days	$5.00
Montana	Full DOB/SSN	Yes	3 days	$8.00
Nevada	Full DOB/SSN	Yes	3 days	$10.00
New Hampshire	Full DOB/SSN	Yes	3 days	$15.00
New Jersey	Full DOB/SSN	Yes	3 days	$18.00
New Mexico	Full DOB/SSN	Yes	3 days	$7.00
North Carolina	Full DOB/SSN	Yes	3 days	$10.00
North Dakota	Full DOB/SSN	Yes	7–14 days	$30.00
Oklahoma	Full DOB/SSN	No	3–7 days	$15.00
Oregon	Full DOB/SSN	Yes	3 days	$8.00
Pennsylvania	Full DOB/SSN	Yes	3 days	$10.00
Rhode Island	Full DOB/SSN	Yes	3 days	$9.00
South Carolina	Full DOB/SSN	No	3 days	$25.00
South Dakota	Full DOB/SSN	Yes	3 days	$20.00
Tennessee	Full DOB/SSN	Yes	3 days	$15.00
Texas	Full DOB/SSN	No	3 days	$5.00
Virginia	Full DOB/SSN	Yes	3 days	$9.00
Washington	Full DOB/SSN	Yes	3 days	$10.00
Wisconsin	Full DOB/SSN	No	3 days	$13.00

* Note, turnaround time, requirements, and access fees may change at any time.

Sex Offender Searches Under Megan's Law

If you work in a home health agency or hospital, send employees into people's homes or expose children to them as in a church or day care a check of the State's sex offenders/child molester database is in order. A criminal search will reveal the sex crime only if you know the county in which the offense occurred and searched that county's records; otherwise, you will never know about the crime unless the sex offender database is checked. Unfortunately, this list is limited to those sex offenders who are registered. Reports have indicated that they may only list half of the reported 386,000 registered sex offenders.

Be sure when conducting this search that the records you review come directly from the state's files. One company offers a database free to employers purported to be "national". After testing this database we found that although it did provide some sex offender information, it was impossible to verify where the information originated as the research found that the database missed a very large percentage (approximately 20%) of registered sex offenders found by searching the actual registries offered by the states themselves. Obviously, anyone who might rely on a "free" database is getting what they are paying for. These types of databases are very dangerous especially if one relies solely on its contents.

Terrorist Searches Now Available

A Terrorist search includes a database from the Office of Foreign Asset Control which was created by the federal Patriot Act. The federal government updates this list of known terrorists and drug traffickers, but provides little in the way of identifiers.

We recommend that you inquire if your Consumer Reporting Agency only searches the OFAC listing for you or searches other databases as well. If your company finds searching OFAC important, you may want to work with a CRA that also searches all of the following: The **OFAC** basic search package should include:

1. **The Terrorist list of Specially Designated Nationals** (SDN) and Blocked Persons as defined by the Office of Foreign Assets Control.
2. **Denied Persons** as supplied by the United States Commerce Department, which indicates individuals and entities restricted from exporting.
3. **OSFI** lists which are supplied by the Canadian Office of the Superintendent of Financial Institutions, containing names of individuals and organizations subject to the Regulations Establishing a list of entities made under subsection 83.0(1) of the Criminal Code of the United Nations Suppression of Terrorism Regulations.
4. **UK Terrorists Lists** which are supplied by the Bank of England.

The **PROHIBITED PARTIES DATABASE SEARCH** is an add-on option. This feature allows you to screen against four government lists of prohibited parties. These lists are:

Debarred Parties—Parties denied export privileges under the International Traffic in Arms Regulations (ITAR) as administered by the Office of Defense Trade Control (DTC).

Denied Persons List—Parties denied export privileges as administered by the Bureau of Industry and Security. The list may be found in the Export Administration Regulations, 15 CFR Part 764 Supplement No. 2.

Entity List—Entities subject to license requirements because of their proliferation of weapons of mass destruction. The list may be found in the Export Administration Regulations, 15 CFR Part 774 Supplement No. 4.

Specially Designated Nationals, Terrorists, Narcotics Traffickers, Blocked Persons and Vessels—Parties subject to various economic sanctioned programs administered by the Office of Foreign Assets Control (OFAC).

The **UNVERIFIED LIST** includes names and countries of foreign persons who in the past were parties to a transaction with respect to which BIS (Bureau of Industry and Security U.S. Department of Commerce) could not conduct a pre-license check ("PLC") or a post-shipment verification ("PSV") for reasons outside of the U.S. Government's control. Any transaction to which a listed person is a party will be deemed by BIS to raise a "red flag" with respect to such transaction within the meaning of the guidance set forth in Supplement No. 3 to 15 C.F.R. Part 732. The "red flag" applies to the person on the Unverified List regardless of where the person is located in the country included on the list.

Database Searches Are Not National

Several companies now advertise a service called a National Criminal Search. Be very cautious as these searches are from a database and not national as advertised.

The National Criminal Database Search is a comprehensive database search and contains millions of offense records including state and county criminal records, many state correctional institution information and several state sex offender lists. It does not, however, include criminal court records from every county and state nor all states correctional or sex offender lists.

The information derived from public record databases may be outdated and/or inaccurate. The National Criminal Database Search should be used as a "conviction locator" only as it may provide additional criminal information not found by researching the county or state of residence or all counties found on the subject's Social Security Trace or Credit Report. When using the National Criminal Database Search, it is crucial to conduct county criminal searches to perform proper due diligence and comply with the law. Identification of individuals is based only upon name and limited identifiers, consequently misidentifications may occur. To search this database, one must provide the full date of birth.

Although now recommended by many CRA's as these databases have been found to be a valuable resource, extreme care must therefore be exercised in the review and use of National Criminal Database Search information and the information should not be used in legal proceedings.

Other Types of Searches

FirstAlert™, is a service offered by InfoLink Screening Services, Inc. at no charge and a few other CRA's at the time a consumer's name and social security number is entered but before the search request is ordered. This service is a very helpful search as it verifies the algorithm of the Social Security Number given by an applicant to determine if the number was issued by the social security department, where it was issued and the approximate year of issue.

Although it is not 100% accurate in its findings, its information can be unexpectedly revealing. For example, it might reveal when an applicant who appears to be about 20 years old claims he lived in your state all his life but a FirstAlert™ search reveals that the Social Security Number he gave you was issued in another state 35 years ago.

For the most part, a **Social Security Trace** will confirm that your applicants are who they say they are, reveal other names used (AKA's) and provide past addresses which can be used to search previous counties of residence.

Every credit bureau offers a SSN Trace report; however all trace reports are not the same. Some companies sell credit headers in bulk and purchasers offer the records as trace reports. These are not always accurate and certainly not up to date. We believe that Trans Union offers the most comprehensive report which they used to call "I.D. Search Plus" (at the time of this writing the name is being changed to "Social Search" or "Social Search Plus"). For a small additional fee they will add their "High Risk Fraud Alert", formally called their "Hawk Alert". Normally this additional fee is not passed along by a CRA to their client. This service identifies any fraud associated with the Social Security Number they have in their files.

A **Motor Vehicle Report** (Driving Record) is inexpensive and recommended for every search because it can reveal information of concern that may not be uncovered in a criminal search. You can learn more about someone's character in a motor vehicle report than most any other report. It reports Driving Under the Influence (DUI's), possession of drugs, current warrants, failures to appear and is an excellent tool to confirm the subject's date of birth as accuracy is critical when researching criminal conviction files.

Where applicants are applying for positions which require driving, a driving record is critical as it also reveals tickets and accidents. One CPA firm added a MVR report to a background check for their receptionist position as one of her duties was to take deposits to the bank. Their first candidate's report revealed several tickets and accidents.

Confirming DOB is critical. Criminals are very aware that often the only identifier in a criminal file is the date of birth. Therefore, they intentionally conceal their true DOB when applying, which makes your criminal file search inaccurate. The MVR report will either confirm that the DOB is theirs or provide you or your CRA with the actual accurate DOB.

You must check applicants' **References**. Some people believe they can't get good information through reference checks, but negligent hiring lawsuits filed against companies that stopped checking references are rampant. (Note: When you outsource references, you must give the applicant a copy of the Federal Trade Commission consumer rights document (§609(c)(3) [§1681g] of the FCRA).

NOTE: It is not unlawful to seek or provide other employers honest and accurate reference information. Further, an employer may also divulge negative information as long as positive information is also offered providing it is truthful and disclosed without malice. Unfortunately in many states employers take the risk of being sued for defamation if negative information is relayed. Although you might win the lawsuit, it is common advice from employment attorneys to not provide any information except dates of employment, position held, and income information. We suggest that you consult with your attorney in this matter and let your conscience be your guide. If you have documented negative behavior and the individual poses a risk of harm to another, seriously consider providing honest and factual information with a truthful statement that you and your company would never consider re-hiring this particular individual.

The Society for Human Resource Management (SHRM) has identified states that have enacted reference-checking bills as Alaska, Arizona, Arkansas, California, Colorado, Delaware, Florida, Georgia, Hawaii, Illinois, Indiana, Iowa, Kansas, Louisiana, Maine, Maryland, Michigan,

Minnesota, Montana, Nevada, North Dakota, Ohio, Oklahoma, Oregon, Rhode Island, South Carolina, South Dakota, Tennessee, Texas, Utah, Virginia and Wyoming. Some state's laws benefit employers and relieve the employer of liability or the possibility of lawsuit when they provide reference information that they believe to be the truth as long as it is in good faith. Malicious behavior or giving information that is knowingly false is never protected. Most states allow for defamation lawsuits, which even if the employer prevails, may cost dearly in attorney's fees.

Unless an applicant's **Credit** can affect your company financially, you shouldn't ask for a credit report as credit may be deemed a privacy issue. When checking credit, make sure you are using one of the credit bureaus' special reports designed for employment, such as Trans Union's "Employment Credit Report" (formally their Pre-Employment Evaluation Report— PEER), Experian's "Employment Insight Report" or Equifax's "Persona". These reports offer most everything within a normal credit report except they (1) don't offer the consumer's date of birth, (2) don't provide credit scores, and (3) they don't place an inquiry on the report that occurs when someone applies for credit as such inquiries affect FICO scores used by lending institutions in making credit determinations.

Education Verification is recommended for managerial positions as for most professional positions. Statistics reveal that education is one of the areas that applicants falsify most often on employment applications. The CRA should verify the "highest degree" attempted or earned (usually college degrees), unless clients specifically ask to verify high school also. The education verification should report the applicant's dates of attendance, graduation date and degree earned. Some educational institutions will report GPA.

An article published in 2004, revealed that six of eleven Georgia teachers reportedly bought advanced degrees from a diploma mill in Liberia. The six Gwinnett County middle-school teachers turned in their letters of resignation in the middle of an investigation by the county's human resource office.

Glynn Cyprien, an assistant coach and on Eddie Sutton's staff, played a key role in helping the Cowboys reach the 2004 final four. Shortly thereafter, he was hired as a basketball coach for the University of Louisiana-Lafayette. Cyprien was later fired as he listed a bachelor's degree from the University of Texas and a master's degree from Lacrosse University. He didn't graduate from UTSA and Lacrosse is an on-line school without accreditation recognized by the Department of Education.

Applicants sometimes lie about their Degrees. Advertisements on the Internet ask: "Do you want a prosperous future and increased money earnings? . . . No one is turned down, . . . earn a diploma from anyplace." Checking licenses and degrees is not difficult and may be outsourced for convenience.

Consumer Reporting Agencies are seeing more and more fake diplomas from fake colleges more commonly known as "diploma mills". A diploma mill (also known as degree mill) is an unaccredited organization which awards "academic degrees" and "diplomas" with little or no academic study and without recognition by any official body. Many diploma mills claim to offer these qualifications on the basis of "life experience", but many only require a payment to issue a qualification. They are used to fraudulently claim academic credentials for use in securing employment.

One such "university" is Columbia State University. InfoLink received a copy of a "Bachelor of Science" degree in Criminal Justice purported to be earned in 1998. Further investigation revealed that the Federal Bureau of Investigation (FBI) actually shut down the operation in 1998 and the former owner and operator was indicted on federal mail fraud charges for running a diploma mill.

Another known mill is Almeda College (aka Almeda University) in Idaho. Their website states that it's not a college in the real sense of the word, but rather a "limited company". The site also clearly states that applicants can earn their degrees based on their life experiences. It also states that there are no books, courses or studying involved in order to obtain a degree.

While there is no official U.S. site that tracks these schools, many states have begun their own. Oregon has a Student Assistance Commission, Office of Degree Authorization that has a comprehensive list of diploma mills which includes Almeda College. According to their office, Almeda has "taken shelter under an Idaho loophole allowing diploma mills if they don't offer degrees to Idaho residents." (see **http://www.osac.state.or.us/oda/unaccredited.html**.)

Employers should confirm any **Professional License** and certification identified by an applicant on their employment application. Reports will reveal the validity of applicants' professional licenses, date of issue, renewal and expiration dates, current status and any disciplinary action.

Sources of Medical License verifications vary by State. However, you may search the following agencies for specific licenses.

- *CNA (Certified Nursing Assistant):* CNA Registraty, Dept. of Public Health, or Dept. of Human Services
- *RN (Registered Nurse):* State Board of Nursing
- *LVN (Licensed Vocational Nurse):* State Board of Nursing
- *MD (Medical Doctor):* State Medical Board of Licensing

Employers in health care should obtain an **OIG Medicare/Medicaid Fraud Report.** The United States Department of Health and Human Services Office of Inspector General (OIG) excludes individuals listed in the Sanction database from working in Medicare, Medicaid and other Federal health care programs. Searches should include the Cumulative Sanction Report and Debarred Contractors List from the General Services Administration. In addition, a search of a licensed practitioner should be made through the National Practitioner Data Bank.

If **Military Service** is important to the position for which you are hiring, a verification of such information can be valuable. The CRA can verify the branch of service and current status.

Often times an employer is concerned about obtaining a Credit Report, but wants information relating to the applicant's character. A search of the index files to identify if the consumer has had any **Liens and Judgments** through a county search may reveal notices of default, county and state tax liens, and unlawful detainers.

Civil Records are requested by organizations seeking to learn if the applicant is litigious. Since services requested for a background check must be job related, there is a concern that civil records are not job related. These records are useful as they reveal lawsuits, unlawful detainers, and restraining orders.

Searches are performed by Plaintiff, Defendant, Attorney, or Case Number of Superior or Multiple Court filings. Generally, civil municipal court records are cases under $25,000. Another reason Civil Searches are generally not recommended is that a search as civil records contain individuals' names only with no other identifiers. Consequently, unless there is an address match in the file, you are never sure that the parties include your applicant.

You may also search the U.S. Federal District Courts for civil cases involving alleged violations of federal statutes or constitutional rights. This can include a national search of U.S. Federal districts excluding Alaska, Guam, Idaho, new Mexico and Northern Marina Islands. Cases may be brought by individuals, companies or governmental entities seeking monetary damages, an injunction, and/or another remedy provided by law. Case information will include the parties name, case title, the court in which the case is located, case number, filing data, nature of suit and closing date.

Workers' Compensation searches are highly recommended in manufacturing and production environments or wherever physical activity such as lifting is part of the job requirement. These searches are also valuable where employers have high workers' compensation claims. This information enables employers to avoid placing employees in positions that may pose risk of re-injury and identify habitual claim filers. Workers' Compensation History is a statewide search available in most states, but must be conducted post-offer.

Employers however, may not rescind an offer merely due to finding a claim and must review the issue to analyze if reasonable accommodations may be made. The primary use of this search is to validate the integrity of the applicant by comparing the employers for which claims were made to the employers the applicant listed on their application. Unfortunately, people "conveniently forget" to list past employers on their application against whom they have filed claims. Employment applications should ask applicants to identify "all" past employers, and a workers' compensation search can catch habitual claimants for falsifying their application when un-reported employers are revealed on their background report.

Workers' Compensation is available in Alaska, Arizona, Arkansas, California, Florida, Idaho, Illinois, Iowa, Kentucky, Louisiana, Maryland, Massachusetts, Michigan, Montana, Nebraska, New Hampshire, North Dakota, Ohio, Okalahoma, Pennsylvania, South Carolina, South Dakota, Tennessee, Vermont, and Wyoming.

California requires prior written approval by the California Department of Industrial Relations, Division of Workers' Compensation Electronic Data Exchange (EDEX). Forms are available through the Consumer Reporting Agency performing the search.

The Following States Require Additional Information

	Full DOB	Signed Release Form	Signed, State-Issued Release Form
Alaska	✔		
Arizona		✔	
Idaho			✔
Massachusetts		✔	
Montana		✔	
New Hampshire		✔	
North Dakota		✔	
Oklahoma			✔
Pennsylvania		✔	
South Carolina		✔	
South Dakota		✔	
Wyoming		✔	

Worker's Compensation Searches are *not available* in the following states: Alabama, Colorado, Connecticut, Delaware, District of Columbia, Georgia, Hawaii, Indiana, Kansas, Maine, Minnesota, Mississippi, Missouri, Nevada, New Jersey, New Mexico, New York, North Carolina, Oregon, Rhode Island, Texas, Utah, Virginia, Washington, West Virginia, and Wisconsin.

Employers may not deny employment to an applicant for whom there is a **current criminal warrant** outstanding. However, employers should suggest that the applicant reapply after clearing the warrant providing documentation of clearance. The same situation occurs when a person is reported to be out on bail pending prosecution. After the applicant goes to court and clears the matter, they should be allowed to bring such documentation back and reapply.

If an applicant is in a **drug rehabilitation program**, don't ask about it. Your consumer reporting agency should not indicate that a consumer is or was in a rehabilitation program in their report because such rehabilitation may fall under the Americans with Disabilities Act and may compromise your position on hiring.

Background Checks: Required by Law

Several industries are required by federal or state mandate to perform background screening. Please review the sections on the various state laws which summarize what you need to know if you are an employer in industries relating to Child Care, Insurance, Elder Care, Health Care, Security, Gaming, or Securities. This section will summarize those industries whereby the federal government is involved.

Banking: The Federal Deposit Insurance Act Section 19

The banking industry is prohibited from hiring any person who has been convicted of any criminal offense involving dishonesty, breach of trust or money laundering; or, has agreed to enter into a pretrial diversion or similar program in connection with a prosecution for such offense. These individuals are prohibited from being associated as an affiliated party with respect to any insured depository institution, to own or control (directly or indirectly) any insured depository institution, participate in any way in the affairs or in a relationship with an insured depository institution.

Aeronautics and Space: The Federal Aviation Administration, Department of Transportation Title 14, Part 107, Sec. 103.31.

The Aviation industry requires specific investigations for individuals who have unescorted access to a security identification display area (SIDA) identified by Section 107.25, others seeking authority to authorize others to have unescorted access to a SIDA, and each airport user (any person making a certification other than an air carrier) and air carrier making a certification to an airport operator.

The requirements include obtaining an employment history consisting of two parts. (1) Obtaining and review of 10 years of employment history and verification of the 5 previous employment years preceding the date of the investigation. (2) Determine if the individual has a criminal record. To satisfy part 2, the criminal record check must not disclose that the individual has been convicted or found not guilty by reason of insanity in any jurisdiction, during the 10 years ending on the date of such investigation of any of the crimes specified in Section 107.31.

Issuance of Hazmat Licenses: Chapter 51 of title 49, United States Code, has been amended with Section 5103a.

A state may not issue to any individual a license to operate a motor vehicle transporting in commerce a hazardous material unless the Secretary of Transportation has first determined that the individual does not pose a security risk. Hazardous materials include (1) any material defined as hazardous material by the Secretary of Transportation; and, (2) any chemical or biological material or agent determined by the Secretary of Health and Human Services or the Attorney General as being a threat to the national security of the United States.

To conform, the state prior to issuing a license must perform a background records check and once performed, notify the Secretary of Transportation of its completion and the results of such check. The scope of the background check shall be a check of all relevant criminal history data bases both domestic and international if appropriate.

Motor Carrier Employers: The United States Department of Transportation's ("DOT") and the Federal Motor Carrier Safety Administration ("FMCSA") maintains regulations concerning information that motor carrier employers must obtain about commercial motor vehicle drivers prior to hire. Specifically, FMCSA has provisions under 49 C.F.R. Part 391, concerning driver qualifications.

Driver-applicants currently are required to provide to prospective employers (among other things, as set forth in 49 C.F.R. § 391.21): (1) a list of the names and addresses of the applicant's employers during the three years preceding the date the application is submitted; (2) the dates he or she was employed by that employer; and, (3) the reason for leaving the employ of each employer. Under FMCSA's revised regulations, applicants also are required, after October 29, 2004, to identify: (a) whether the applicant was subject to the FMCSA's rules and regulations while employed by the previous employers he or she identified; and (b) whether any of those previous jobs were designated as "safety-sensitive" by any DOT operating agency and subject to DOT's drug and alcohol testing requirements, set forth at 49 C.F.R. Part 40.

The prospective employer must investigate, at a minimum, the following information from all previous employers that employed the driver to operate a commercial motor vehicle within the previous three years: (i) general driver identification and employment verification information; and, (ii) certain information about accidents involving the driver.

The prospective employer also must investigate the following information from all previous DOT-regulated employers that employed the driver to perform any safety-sensitive functions, that required drug and alcohol testing under 49 C.F.R. Part 40, within the previous three years: (i) whether, within the previous three years, the driver had violated DOT's or FMCSA's drug and alcohol prohibitions; (ii) for a driver reported to have violated DOT's or FMCSA's drug and alcohol prohibitions within the last three years, whether the driver failed to undertake or complete a rehabilitation program prescribed by a substance abuse professional ("SAP"). If the previous employer does not know this information (e.g., where the employer terminated a driver who tested positive on a drug test), the prospective employer must obtain documentation of the driver's successful completion of the SAP's referral directly from the driver; (iii) for a driver reported to have violated DOT's or FMCSA's drug and alcohol prohibitions who successfully completed a SAP's rehabilitation referral, and remained in the employ of the referring employer, information on whether the driver had the following testing violations subsequent to completion of a SAP referral:

(A) Alcohol tests with a result of 0.04 or higher alcohol concentration;
(B) Verified positive drug tests;
(C) Refusals to test (including verified adulterated or substituted drug test results);

The previous employer must take all precautions reasonably necessary to ensure the accuracy of the records. The previous employer also must provide specific contact information in case a driver chooses to correct or rebut the data. Finally, the previous employer must keep records of all requests for information and the responses for one year, including the date, the party to whom it was released, and a summary identifying what was provided.

A prospective employer must provide to the previous employer the driver's written consent for the release of the above-listed information. If the driver refuses to provide written consent, the prospective employer must not permit the driver to operate a commercial motor vehicle. Previous employers must respond to requests for the information listed above within 30 days after the request is received. If there is no safety performance history information to report for that driver, previous employers nonetheless are required to send a response confirming the non-existence of any such data.

Before an application is submitted, the motor carrier employer must inform the applicant that the information he or she has provided may be used, and the applicant's previous employers will be contacted, for the purpose of investigating the applicant's safety performance history information as required by the newly-revised 49 C.F.R. § 391.23. The prospective employer must also notify the driver in writing of his or her "due process" rights regarding information received as a result of these investigations. Specifically, the prospective employer must expressly notify drivers with DOT-regulated employment during the preceding three years—via the application form or other written document prior to any hiring decision—that he or she has the following rights regarding the investigative information that will be provided to the prospective employer: (1) the right to review information provided by previous employers; (2) the right to have errors in the information corrected by the previous employer and for that previous employer to re-send the corrected information to the prospective employer; and, (3) the right to have a rebuttal statement attached to the alleged erroneous information, if the previous employer and the driver cannot agree on the accuracy of the information.

Drivers Privacy Protection Act

18 U.S.C. § 2721 et. seq.
(Public Law 103-322)

Section 2721. Prohibition on release and use of certain personal information from State motor vehicle records

(a) In General—Except as provided in subsection (b), a State department of motor vehicles, and any officer, employee, or contractor, thereof, shall not knowingly disclose or otherwise make available to any person or entity personal information about any individual obtained by the department in connection with a motor vehicle record.

(b) Permissible Uses—Personal information referred to in subsection (a) shall be disclosed for use in connection with matters of motor vehicle or driver safety and theft, motor vehicle emissions, motor vehicle product alterations, recalls, or advisories, performance monitoring of motor vehicles and dealers by motor vehicle manufacturers, and removal of non-owner records from the original owner records of motor vehicle manufacturers to carry out the purposes of the *Automobile Information Disclosure Act,* the *Motor Vehicle Information and Cost Saving Act,* the *National Traffic and Motor Vehicle Safety Act of 1966,* the *Anti-Car Theft Act of 1992,* and the *Clean Air Act,* and may be disclosed as follows:

(1) For use by any government agency, including any court or law enforcement agency, in carrying out its functions, or any private person or entity acting on behalf of a Federal, State, or local agency in carrying out its functions.

(2) For use in connection with matters of motor vehicle or driver safety and the motor vehicle emissions; motor vehicle product alterations, recalls, or advisories; performance monitoring of motor vehicles, motor vehicle parts and dealers; motor vehicle market research activities, including survey research; and removal of non-owner records from the original owner records of motor vehicle manufacturers.

(3) For use in the normal course of business by a legitimate business or its agents, employees, or contractors, but only —

    (A) to verify the accuracy of personal information submitted by the individual to the business or its agents, employees, or contractors; and

    (B) if such information as so submitted is not correct or is no longer correct, to obtain the correct information, but only for the purposes of preventing fraud by, pursuing legal remedies against, or recovering on a debt or security interest against, the individual.

(4) For use in connection with any civil, criminal, administrative, or arbitral proceeding in any Federal, State, or local court or agency or before any self-regulatory body, including the service of process, investigation in anticipation of litigation, and the execution or enforcement of judgments and orders, or pursuant to an order of a Federal, State, or local court.

(5) For use in research activities, and for use in producing statistical reports, so long as the personal information is not published, redisclosed, or used to contact individuals.

(6) For use by any insurer or insurance support organization, or by a self-insured entity, or its agents, employees, or contractors, in connection with claims investigation activities, anti-fraud activities, rating or underwriting.

(7) For use in providing notice to the owners of towed or impounded vehicles.

(8) For use by any licensed private investigative agency or licensed security service for any purpose permitted under this subsection.

(9) For use by an employer or its agents or insurer to obtain or verify information relating to a holder of a commercial driver's license that is required under the *Commercial Motor Vehicle Safety Act of 1986* (49 U.S.C. App. 2710 et seq.).

(10) For use in connection with the operation of private toll transportation facilities.

(11) For any other use in response to requests for individual motor vehicle records if the motor vehicle department has provided in a clear and conspicuous manner on forms for issuance or renewal of operator's permits, titles, registrations, or identification cards, notice that personal information collected by the department may be disclosed to any business or person, and has provided in a clear and conspicuous manner on such forms an opportunity to prohibit such disclosures.

(12) For bulk distribution for surveys, marketing or solicitations if the motor vehicle department has implemented methods and procedures to ensure that—(A) individuals are provided an opportunity, in a clear and conspicuous manner, to prohibit such uses; and (B) the information will be used, rented, or sold solely for bulk distribution for surveys, marketing, and solicitations, and that surveys, marketing, and solicitations will not be directed at those individuals who have requested in a timely fashion that they not be directed at them.

(13) For use by any requester, if the requester demonstrates it has obtained the written consent of the individual to whom the information pertains.

(14) For any other use specifically authorized under the law of the State that holds the record, if such use is related to the operation of a motor vehicle or public safety.

(c) Resale or Re-disclosure—An authorized recipient of personal information (except recipient under subsection (b)(11) or (12)) may resell or redisclose the information only for a use permitted under subsection (b) (but not for uses under subsection (b)(11) or (12)). An authorized recipient under subsection (b)(11) may resell or redisclose personal information for any purpose. An authorized recipient under subsection (b)(12) may resell or redisclose personal information pursuant to subsection (b)(12). Any authorized recipient (except a recipient under subsection (b)(11)) that resells or rediscloses personal information covered by this title must keep for a period of 5 years records identifying each person or entity that receives information and the permitted purpose for which the information will be used and must make such records available to the motor vehicle department upon request.

(d) Waiver Procedures—A State motor vehicle department may establish and carry out procedures under which the department or its agents, upon receiving a request for personal information that does not fall within one of the exceptions in subsection (b), may mail a copy of the request to the individual about whom the information was requested, informing such individual of the request, together with a statement to the effect that the information will not be released unless the individual waives such individual's right to privacy under this section.

Section 2722. Additional unlawful acts

(a) Procurement for Unlawful Purpose—It shall be unlawful for any person knowingly to obtain or disclose personal information, from a motor vehicle record, for any use not permitted under section 2721(b) of this title.

(b) False Representation—It shall be unlawful for any person to make false representation to obtain any personal information from an individual's motor vehicle record.

Section 2723. Penalties

(a) Criminal Fine—A person who knowingly violates this chapter shall be fined under this title.

(b) Violations by State Department of Motor Vehicles—Any State department of motor vehicles that has a policy or practice of substantial noncompliance with this chapter shall be subject to a civil penalty imposed by the Attorney General of not more than $5,000 a day for each day of substantial noncompliance.

Section 2724. Civil action

(a) Cause of Action—A person who knowingly obtains, discloses or uses personal information, from a motor vehicle record, for a purpose not permitted under this chapter shall be liable to the individual to whom the information pertains, who may bring a civil action in a United States district court.

(b) Remedies—The court may award—
(1) actual damages, but not less than liquidated damages in the amount of$2,500;
(2) punitive damages upon proof of willful or reckless disregard of the law;
(3) reasonable attorneys' fees and other litigation costs reasonably incurred; and
(4) such other preliminary and equitable relief as the court determines to be appropriate.

Section 2725. Definitions

In this chapter—

(1) "motor vehicle record" means any record that pertains to a motor vehicle operator's permit, motor vehicle title, motor vehicle registration, or identification card issued by a department of motor vehicles;

(2) "person" means an individual, organization or entity, but does not include a State or agency thereof; and

(3) "personal information" means information that identifies an individual, including an individual's photograph, social security number, driver identification number, name, address (but not the 5-digit zip code), telephone number, and medical or disability information, but does not include information on vehicular accidents, driving violations, and driver's status.

7 Free Steps Any Employer Can Take Immediately

There are a number of steps that an employer can take immediately to protect against making a bad hire.

1) Place prominent signs around your company that state you conduct background checks and drug testing. Having a sign is very similar to the security alarm sign you might have at your home or office that deters unlawful individuals from entering. Publicizing the fact that you pre-screen new hires is a great way to deter people who won't pass the background check from applying for employment and wasting your time and money. Many (but not all) applicants with criminal convictions and falsified resumes will not apply because they know that they'll be screened out in the hiring process. These signs also make your employees and the public feel safer on company premises.

2) Place a notice on your Web site that you perform background checks and drug testing. It deters undesirable applicants like the signs on your physical premises. Applicants who visit your web site for employment information will see that you promote a safe working environment, which is an excellent employee benefit!

3) When advertising for a job opening, place the following words after the ad: "Background Checks required!" The addition of these 3 words will save you thousands of dollars and many hours as individuals with a questionable past will not apply and waist your time.

4) When outsourcing background screening you are required to have the applicant sign a disclosure and authorization document prior to the background check request. Even if you don't outsource background screening, create an ominous looking disclosure and authorization form for background checks and drug tests. Give these forms to all applicants before they complete your employment applications. If applicants have something to hide, your forms will make them think twice about completing the application process.

5) Advise all applicants that your company performs background checks and obtain their authorization in advance. Write a background screening policy and distribute it to all employees. In your policy list the required searches for each job position inferring that promotions are based on the satisfactory response from a background check. It is important that employees know that you conduct background checks and "may" perform post-hire searches. Once your policy is complete, distribute disclosure forms to all employees and ask for their signature in advance.

As a side note: one InfoLink client announced to his current employees that the company was instituting a program of background checks and he passed around disclosure forms for all to sign. Seven employees resigned on the spot. He was thrilled as he saved the cost of background checks on all 7 who obviously wouldn't pass.

6) Insist that your temporary employment agency perform criminal background checks and get a copy of the background screening report prior to employing any temp. Applicants with criminal records frequently work through temporary agencies since many do not conduct criminal background checks. It is important that you protect your company by having the agency screen the candidates they send you so you can have peace of mind. As you are a "party in interest" make sure the disclosure form authorizes you to a copy of every report.

7) Require vendors and independent contractors who come on to your premises to criminal background check their employees. This requirement costs you nothing and protects your employees, customers, and the public. Create a policy indicating what they should check. Insist that your vendor sign off that each criminal background check was completed and reviewed before they send their representative to your location and require audit rights.

Bonus

Have a complete employment application that asks all the questions you can legally ask. Put a large notice at the top of your application that says you perform background checks and drug testing. Use your application form as a deterrent reminding everyone that they will have a background check. The federal Equal Employment Opportunities Commission (EEOC) has listed several questions that can be legally asked prior to making an offer of employment. Include the ones relevant to you on your application. We recommend you visit www.great hire.com and order their "Perfect Application & More" CD-Rom Suite.

NOTE: Some organizations only fingerprint applicants. Although a disclosure form is not required under these circumstances, we still recommend you offer an ominous disclosure form as a deterrent. This one idea may save you thousands of dollars in saved fees and time.

Employment Applications

A comprehensive employment application form is essential. Studies show that 20–30% of employment application information from applicants is falsified. Companies and hiring managers must be knowledgeable about all potential new employees!

State and federal labor and employment laws are becoming more restrictive for employers relative to what you may ask job applicants, and the penalties for violations are getting more costly. Lawsuits concerning improper questions about past criminal history, equal employment opportunity issues and others—within employment applications and interviews—are on the rise. Fines ranging from $200-$500, actual damages, plus legal fees are awarded on a regular basis.

The best applications add the fact that you may do a background check on the front of the application, not in small type on the back. A prominent box on the front of the report form indicating, "We are concerned about violence in the workplace, falsified employment applications and theft. We will conduct background checks on every candidate for employment" is an excellent deterrent. Place a separate box on your application for drug screening, even if you only do it on reasonable suspicion.

Have your application ask about criminal convictions as follows:

Please respond to the following questions in the most complete and accurate manner possible. Do not identify convictions for which the criminal record has been expunged or sealed by the court; or, misdemeanor convictions for which any probation has been completed and the case dismissed by the court. Furthermore, please note that no applicant will be denied employment solely on the grounds that they have been charged, committed, or convicted of (or pleaded guilty or no contest to) a criminal offense; or, solely on an affirmative answer. The nature, date, surrounding circumstances, and relevance of the offense to the position(s) applied for will be considered.

Have you ever, under your name or another name, been convicted of (or pleaded guilty or no contest to) a felony or misdemeanor?   ❐ Yes   ❐ No

Have you ever, under your name or another name, been convicted of a crime which resulted in your being in prison and/or jail and released from prison and/or jail or paroled? ❐ Yes   ❐ No

If yes to either question noted above, please fully explain when, where and of what you were convicted and the result of the case(s):

_____

_____

Are you currently under arrest, or released on bond on your own recognizance, pending trial for a criminal offense?   ❐ Yes   ❐ No

If yes, state the nature of the crime charged, and when and where the trial is pending:

_____

_____

Have you used illegal drugs in the last six months?   ❐ Yes   ❐ No

Do you take any illegal drugs or medications which have not been prescribed for you? ❐ Yes   ❐ No

If yes to either of the above questions, when was the last time you used illegal drugs?

Please explain: _____

Have you ever been convicted of driving under the influence (DUI)? ❐ Yes ❐ No

Do you use alcohol to the extent that it would impair your job performance?
❐ Yes ❐ No

If a job description has been provided to you, are you able to perform the essential functions of the job you are applying for (with or without reasonable accommodation)?
❐ Yes ❐ No

If no, describe the functions that cannot be performed:

_____

_____

Certain states have restrictions on what can be reported or how to ask regarding past criminal activity. Please review what is allowed in the following states and amend your application to conform.

CA   Do not provide or ask for information concerning:
   (1) any conviction for which the record has been judicially ordered sealed, expunged or statutorily eradicated; or,
   (2) any misdemeanor conviction for which probation has been completed or discharged and the case has been judicially dismissed; or,
   (3) Pursuant to Section 432.8 of the California Labor Code, please do not provide any information concerning misdemeanor or infraction marijuana convictions that occurred more than two years from today's date and specifically HS11357(b) or (c), HS11360(b), HS11364, HS11365, or HS11550 as they related to marijuana before January 1, 1976 and their statutory predecessors.

THE FOLLOWING SECTION IS FOR EMPLOYMENT WITHIN THE HEALTH CARE INDUSTRY IN CALIFORNIA

Please answer the following only if:

1. The position for which you are applying will provide you access to patients. Have you ever been arrested for a sex related crime? ❏ Yes ❏ No

Please Explain: _____

_____

2. The position for which you are applying will provide you access to drugs or medications. Have you ever been arrested for a drug related crime? ❏ Yes ❏ No

Please Explain: _____

_____

CT   Per Public Act No. 02-136 you must add the following words in the section which asks about criminal convictions:

"Pursuant to Connecticut Public Act No. 02-136 and specifically Section 31-51i of the general statutes; I understand that I am not required to disclose the existence of any arrest, criminal charge or conviction, the records of which have been erased pursuant to section 46b-146, 54-76o, or 54-142a; that criminal records subject to erasure pursuant to section 46b-146, 54-76o or 54-142a are records pertaining to a finding of delinquency or that a child was a member of a family with service needs, an adjudication as a youthful offender, a criminal charge that has been dismissed or annulled, a criminal charge for which the person has been found not guilty or a conviction for which the person received an absolute pardon; and, that any person whose criminal records have been erased pursuant to section 46b-146, 54-76o or 54-142a shall be deemed to have never been arrested within the meaning of the general statutes with respect to the proceedings so erased and may so swear under oath."

IL   As of 1/1/2004, Section 12(a) of the Criminal Identification Act requires applications for employment must state: "applicants are not obligated to disclose sealed or expunged records of conviction or arrests".

MA   Have you ever been convicted of a felony? ❏ Yes   ❏ No Record
If so, when? _____

Within the last five years have you been convicted of or released from incarceration for a misdemeanor, which was not a first offense for drunkenness, simple assault, speeding, a minor traffic violation, an affray or disturbing the peace?
❒ Yes ❒ No Record

(A criminal conviction will not necessarily be a bar to employment. To help us evaluate your application, please describe the nature of the crime and your subsequent rehabilitation.)

In Massachusetts, an application for employment with a sealed record on file with the commissioner of probation may answer "No Record" with respect to any inquiry herein relative to prior arrests, criminal court appearances or convictions. An applicant for employment with a sealed record on file with the commissioner of probation may answer "No Record" to an inquiry herein relative to prior arrests or criminal court appearances. In addition, any applicant for employment may answer "No Record" with respect to any inquiry relative to prior arrests, court appearances and adjudications in all cases of delinquency or as a child in need of services which did not result in a complaint transferred to the superior court for criminal prosecution.

NV	Only report those convictions that occurred within the past seven (7) years.
NH	Only report those convictions that have taken place in the past seven (7) years. Convictions, which have not been annulled, will not necessarily disqualify you from employment
OR	Do not provide information concerning a juvenile record that has been expunged.
SD	Have you been convicted of a felony?
WA	Limit your answer to convictions for which the date of conviction or prison release, whichever is more recent, is within seven (7) years of today's date.

Don't get hung out to dry. References are just not enough! You've got to do background screening; you've got to check out applicants today in every possible way.

Questions and Answers

Question: How can I get a copy of InfoLink's' employment application?

Answer: Visit www.great hire.com. You can purchase the Perfect Application & More suite. It not only has the most comprehensive application ever created with state specific requirements; but, it also has sample letters, an affirmative action form, an arbitration form, and drug and alcohol release, 204 interview questions, job denial letters and more.

Question: Where does liability fall when an executive search firm does the checking?

Answer: The FCRA says that executive search firms don't have to disclose whether or not they performed an investigative consumer report (reference check) if they are hiring a person for you. But because the new hire will be your employee, you should either do the background check or insist that the executive search firm do it.

The disclosure form should clearly state that whoever asks for or performs the background check may share the resulting information with others who have a need to know. You have a need to know the information revealed and the party checking needs to be authorized to share it with you.

Question: If you are recruiting, do you have to supply all applicants with a copy of their report?

Answer: No, only if they request a copy or before taking adverse action.

Question: Who should check an applicant's references?

Answer: References need to be handled by someone who has the time to check them. The problem with reference checks is that employers and references play a lot of phone tag and by the time they finally talk to each other neither one has time to talk. Outsourcing reference checking to a company that specializes in it provides much faster and more professional responses.

Question: When taking adverse action, do you have to be specific as to why you are not hiring the person?

Answer: NO, adverse action only requires that you indicate that your decision is based in whole or in part on the information contained within the report. you don't have to tell the person what information caused you to make your decision.

Question: If you are applying for a job and have something on your record, what do you recommend?

Answer: We recommend that you be honest on your application as often times the fact that you were honest in advance trumps the actual negative history. Employers may forgive the past if it doesn't pose a threat to the present.

Question: If I have a specific question, what source do you recommend I contact for an answer?

Answer: We recommend that you look at the website: www.allexperts.com. You will find several categories to choose from that may serve your need for information.

State Laws and Suggested State Reviews

State laws vary regarding pre-employment inquires, fair credit, labor and employment. In addition, several states have specific laws regarding privacy, civil rights, and background screening involving children, financial institutions or law enforcement which are not noted or simply summarized herein as space does not permit great detail. Please note that occasionally state Web site links change and though the author has attempted to provide the latest resource information available at the time of publication, this information is subject to change.

Further, please note that the information on state laws is information that is available and valid as of the date of this writing. It may not be complete and is subject to change. Readers should consult with legal counsel within the jurisdiction to obtain updates and legal advice before relying on this information or make changes in practice or policy.

Twenty-four states have enacted laws specific to background checks and various states have privacy and civil rights laws.

Various states require background screening through fingerprinting for positions within school districts, home health care, nursing, government, social services, etc. The following state listing includes some reference to such state requirements.

Regarding "Searches Available": Although State Repository records may be available, access to such records may be by fingerprinting only, by mail which takes an unreasonable period of time, with special forms, notarized signatures, with additional identifiers, or in person only by the employer.

Here are some specific state guidelines and laws to review:

Alabama

CODE OF ALABAMA
- Title 25. Industrial Relations And Labor. Chapter 1. General Provisions.
  - Article 3. Age Discrimination By Employers Prohibited
  - Article 4. Use Of Consumer Reporting Agencies
- Title 22. Health, Mental Health And Environmental Control.
  - Subtitle 1. Health And Environmental Control Generally.
  - Article 2. Employee Background Investigations
  - Article 4. Criminal History Information
- Alabama defines a "CRA" and a "User" of information from a CRA
- Criminal history background checks are required for employees of public and non public schools and licensed or approved child and adult care facilities.

SEARCHES AVAILABLE
- County Court Searches
- Sexual Offender
- Incarceration Records
- State Repository* (notarized release)

Alaska

Alaska has guidelines for pre-employment inquiries. You may access the Alaska Department of Labor and Workforce Development Employer Handbook, "Pre-Employment Questioning" found at http://www.labor.state.ak.us/handbook/legal7.htm.

Please Also Review:
- Title 18. Health, Safety, and Housing. Chapter 80. State Commission for Human Rights. Article 4. Discriminatory Practices Prohibited. Sec. 18.80.210 Civil rights, Sec. 18.80.220 Unlawful employment practices; exception
- Title 18. Health, Safety, and Housing. Chapter 20. Hospitals and Nursing Facilities. Article 4. Nursing Facilities
- Prior to the issuance of a teaching certificate by the education department, applicants are required to undergo a criminal background check.
- Persons applying for a license to drive a school bus for the public school system must submit information sufficient to complete a background check, including a fingerprint check.
- Nursing homes and assisted living homes may not employ an individual unless the individual, before beginning employment, provides to the facility (1) a sworn statement as to whether he has been convicted of an offense listed in the department's regulations, (2) the results of a name-check criminal background investigation that was completed by the Department of Public Safety no more than 30 days before he is hired, and (3) two full sets of his fingerprints. The facility must submit the fingerprints to the Department of Public Safety within 30 days after hiring, to be sent to the Federal Bureau of Investigation for a national criminal history record check.

SEARCHES AVAILABLE
- County Court Searches
- Sexual Offender
- Incarceration Records
- State Repository* (fingerprints)
- Workers' Compensation Records

Arizona

ARIZONA STATUTES
- Title 20. Insurance, Chapter 11. Insurance Information And Privacy Protection, Article 1. General Provisions
- Title 44. Trade And Commerce, Chapter 11. Regulations Concerning Particular Businesses, Article 6. Consumer Reporting Agencies And Fair Credit Reporting
  - *Arizona Rev. Stat. 44.1691.14.1696*

- *Arizona Rev. Stat. 44.1693.14.1696*
1. *§ 44-1691. Definitions*
   - "Consumer report" means any written, oral, or other communication of any information by a consumer reporting agency bearing on a consumer's credit worthiness, credit standing, credit capacity, character, general reputation, personal characteristics, or mode of living which is used or expected to be used or collected in whole or in part for the purpose of serving as a factor in establishing the consumer's eligibility for (b) Employment purposes,
   - "Employment purposes" when used in connection with a consumer report means a report used for the purpose of evaluating a consumer for employment, promotion, reassignment or retention as an employee.
     1) Adverse underwriting decisions
     2) Consumer credit reports
     3) Lists Permissible Purposes of consumer reports §44-1692
     4) Access to reports
2. *§ 44-1695. Liability*
   a) A consumer reporting agency or information source is not liable to any consumer resulting from reporting inaccurate information corrected in compliance with § 44-1694 except as provided in this section.
   b) A consumer reporting agency is liable for any damages and attorney fees and court costs that are incurred by a consumer and that result from reporting of inaccurate information that a consumer reporting agency refuses to correct as provided in § 44-1694.
   c) Any consumer reporting agency, user of information or source of information that is grossly negligent in the use or preparation of a consumer report or who acts willfully and maliciously with intent to harm a consumer is liable to the consumer for actual damages, if any, punitive damages and attorney fees and court costs.
   d) If a consumer reporting agency prepares a consumer report, the consumer reporting agency shall follow reasonable procedures to assure the maximum possible accuracy of the information relating to the consumer who is the subject of the consumer report.

- *Arizona Rev. Stat. § 13904(E)*
  Unless the offense has a reasonable relationship to the occupation, an occupational license may not be denied solely on the basis of a felony or misdemeanor conviction.

- Also See: Title 41. State Government, Chapter 12. Public Safety, Article 3.1. Fingerprinting Division

- Criminal records checks are required for persons employed in the following agencies and programs: (1) juvenile offender programs; (2) children's behavioral health programs; (3) developmental disability contract providers and home- and community-based service providers; (4) child care facility license applicants, employees and volunteers; (5) child care group home certificate applicants, employees and volunteers; (6) shelters for victims of domestic violence; (7) residential and nursing care institutions and home health agencies; and (8) school district certificated personnel, non-certificated personnel and people who are not paid district employees, information technology personnel.
- Fingerprinting is required for criminal background checks as a condition of employment in the following: juvenile delinquent probation officers; noncertificated personnel initially hired by any school district; school officers and employees of the state school for the deaf and blind; children's behavioral health services employees; child care personnel; day care group home personnel; state-employed juvenile correction facility employees; corrections officer and employees; social service officers and employees; and child care good program employees.

SEARCHES AVAILABLE
- County Court Searches
- Sexual Offender
- Incarceration Records
- State Repository* (fingerprints required)
- Workers' Compensation Records

Arkansas

ARKANSAS CODE OF 1987
- Title 4. Business And Commercial Law, Subtitle 7. Consumer Protection, Chapter 93. Credit Reporting Disclosures
  - Definitions: the terms "consumer", "consumer report", "consumer reporting agency", and "person" have the same meaning as used in the federal Fair Credit Reporting Act
  - Adverse action
    (a) The notification of adverse action shall be in writing and shall contain:
      (1) A statement of the action taken;
      (2) The name and address of the creditor;
      (3) The name and address of the consumer reporting agency making the report; and
      (4) The social security number of the consumer, provided that the social security number has been given to the user of the consumer report by the consumer or is contained in the consumer report received from the consumer reporting agency.

(b) Any person who fails to provide the notification required by this chapter shall be liable to the injured party for actual damages.

- Criminal record checks are required for employment in counseling, psychology, social work, care for the elderly and individuals with disabilities, employment with a state agency involving contact with children, child welfare agencies and employment of criminal offenders.
- All employees or conditional employees in licensed child care facilities or facilities operating with a church-operated exemption will be matched against records maintained by the Arkansas child abuse central registry for reports of child maltreatment. The background checks must occur prior to hire and every two years after hire. The child care facility review board may deny a license or church-operated exemption to any applicant found to have any record of child maltreatment. In the event that a legible set of fingerprints cannot be obtained after a minimum of three attempts, the review board will determine eligibility based on a name check.
- Without proof of rehabilitation, no person is eligible to be a child care facility owner, operator or employee in a licensed or church-operated exempt facility if that person has been found guilty of any of a list of felonies or misdemeanors involving violence or sexual misconduct.
- Mandatory criminal background checks are required for ElderChoice providers— individuals and entities that provide services in the homes of individuals and that are designated by the state Division of Aging and Adult Services as ElderChoice providers.
- Criminal background checks are mandated for persons who provide care to the elderly or to individuals with disabilities, when the workers are placed by a private placement agency or contract staffing agency. The private placement or contracting agency is responsible for initiating the criminal background check.

SEARCHES AVAILABLE

- County Court Searches
- Sexual Offender
- Incarceration Records
- State Repository* (Bureau's request form)
- Workers' Compensation Records

California

California Labor Code § 432.7

- Employers may not ask about an arrest that did not lead to conviction; may not ask about pretrial or post-trial diversion programs. May ask about arrest if prospective employee is awaiting trial. May not ask about a marijuana conviction more than 2 years old.
- Convictions. May ask about conviction even if no sentence is imposed.

- "nor shall any employer seek from any source whatsoever, or utilize, as a factor in determining any condition of employment including hiring, promotion, termination, or any apprenticeship training program or any other training program leading to employment, any record of arrest or detention that did not result in conviction, or any record regarding a referral to, and participation in, any pretrial or post-trial diversion program."
- Employers in health care can ask about "arrests" for drug related crimes if the subject would have access to drugs or medications and they may ask about a sex related crime if they have access to patients.

Department of Fair Employment and Housing
- "Pre-Employment Inquiry Guidelines" found at: http://cit.hr.caltech.edu/policies/PM/pm9-5.html or www.csulb.edu/depts/oed/resources/pub3b.htm
- "it is unlawful for an employer or other covered entity to inquire or seek information about an applicant that concerns any arrest or detention not resulting in conviction"

California Civil Code
- California Consumers Credit Reporting Agencies Act 1785.1-1785.30
  - §1785.15(f) This section requires the CRA provide specific language explaining the consumers' rights should a consumer request a copy of their credit report in California. The section specifically begins as: "Any written disclosure [by a CRA] must conform by providing a consumer their rights. In order to comply, it is sufficient if such disclosure is in substantially the following form ". . ." (Please review this section for the exact language which when in 11 point type extends to a full 8 by 11 piece of paper.)
  - §1785.20.5 requires that the disclosure form inform the person that a report will be used, provide the source of the report, and contain a box that the person may check off to receive a copy of the credit report
- California Consumers Investigative Reporting Agencies Act 1786.1-1786.56
  - §1786.16(a). Any person who requests a consumer report for employment purposes shall not procure or cause to be prepared an investigative consumer report unless the following applicable conditions are met:
    - (2) If, at any time, an investigative consumer report is sought for employment purposes other than suspicion of wrongdoing or misconduct by the subject of the investigation, the person seeking the investigative consumer report may procure the report, or cause the report to be made, only if all of the following apply:
      - (A) The person procuring or causing the report to be made has a permissible purpose.
      - (B) The person procuring or causing the report to be made provides a clear and conspicuous disclosure in writing to the consumer at any time before the report is procured or caused to be made in a document that consists solely of the disclosure, that:

    (i) An investigative consumer report may be obtained.

    (ii) The permissible purpose of the report is identified.

    (iii) The disclosure may include information on the consumer's character, general reputation, personal characteristics, and mode of living.

    (iv) Identifies the name, address, and telephone number of the investigative consumer reporting agency conducting the investigation.

    (v) Notifies the consumer in writing of the nature and scope of the investigation requested, including a summary of the provisions of Section 1786.22.

  (C) The consumer has authorized in writing the procurement of the report.

(b) Any person described above shall do the following:

  (1) Provide the consumer a means by which the consumer may indicate on a written form, by means of a box to check, that the consumer wishes to receive a copy of any report that is prepared. If the consumer wishes to receive a copy of the report, the recipient of the report shall send a copy of the report to the consumer within three business days of the date that the report is provided to the recipient, who may contract with any other entity to send a copy to the consumer. The notice to request the report may be contained on either the disclosure form, as required by subdivision (a), or a separate consent form. The copy of the report shall contain the name, address, and telephone number of the person who issued the report and how to contact them.

  (2) Comply with Section 1786.40, if the taking of adverse action is a consideration.

(c) Subdivisions (a) and (b) do not apply to an investigative consumer report procured or caused to be prepared by an employer, if the report is sought for employment purposes due to suspicion held by an employer of wrongdoing or misconduct by the subject of the investigation.

• 1786.18 (a) Except as authorized under subdivision (b), an investigative consumer reporting agency may not make or furnish any investigative consumer report containing any of the following items of information:

  (7) Records of arrest, indictment, information, misdemeanor complaint, or conviction of a crime that, from the date of disposition, release, or parole, antedate the report by more than seven years. These items of information shall no longer be reported if at any time it is learned that, in the case of a conviction, a full pardon has been granted or, in the case of an arrest, indictment, information, or misdemeanor complaint, a conviction did not result; except that records of arrest, indictment, information, or misdemeanor complaints may be reported pending pronouncement of judgment on the particular subject matter of those records.

- 1786.20. (b) Whenever an investigative consumer reporting agency prepares an investigative consumer report, it shall follow reasonable procedures to assure maximum possible accuracy of the information concerning the individual about whom the report relates.
- 1786.22 (a) An investigative consumer reporting agency shall supply files and information required under Section 1786.10 during normal business hours and on reasonable notice.

    (b) Files maintained on a consumer shall be made available for the consumer's visual inspection, as follows:

        (1) In person, if he appears in person and furnishes proper identification. A copy of his file shall also be available to the consumer for a fee not to exceed the actual costs of duplication services provided.

        (2) By certified mail, if he makes a written request, with proper identification, for copies to be sent to a specified addressee. Investigative consumer reporting agencies complying with requests for certified mailings under this section shall not be liable for disclosures to third parties caused by mishandling of mail after such mailings leave the investigative consumer reporting agencies.

        (3) A summary of all information contained in files on a consumer and required to be provided by Section 1786.10 shall be provided by telephone, if the consumer has made a written request, with proper identification for telephone disclosure, and the toll charge, if any, for the telephone call is prepaid by or charged directly to the consumer.

    (c) The term "proper identification" as used in subdivision (b) shall mean that information generally deemed sufficient to identify a person. Such information includes documents such as a valid driver's license, social security account number, military identification card, and credit cards. Only if the consumer is unable to reasonably identify himself with the information described above, may an investigative consumer reporting agency require additional information concerning the consumer's employment and personal or family history in order to verify his identity.

    (d) The investigative consumer reporting agency shall provide trained personnel to explain to the consumer any information furnished him pursuant to Section 1786.10.

    (e) The investigative consumer reporting agency shall provide a written explanation of any coded information contained in files maintained on a consumer. This written explanation shall be distributed whenever a file is provided to a consumer for visual inspection as required under Section 1786.22.

    (f) The consumer shall be permitted to be accompanied by one other person of his choosing, who shall furnish reasonable identification. An investigative consumer reporting agency may require the consumer to furnish a written statement granting permission to the consumer reporting agency to discuss the consumer's file in such person's presence.

- 1786.28 (b) items of public record relating to arrests, indictments, convictions, suits, tax liens, and outstanding judgments shall be considered up to date if the current public record status of the item at the time of the report is reported.
- Employers may inquire about arrest records when applicants are applying for criminal justice positions, to operate businesses on public lands and for jobs with access to patients, drugs or medication.
- Employers may obtain conviction and arrest records from the Department of Justice for any prospective employee who applies for a license, employment or volunteer position that would involve supervisory or disciplinary power over minors and others.
- Employers are required to inform parents or guardians, at least 10 days prior to the start date, of prospective employees or volunteers who have a criminal record reflecting sexual offenses, revealed through a criminal background check with the aid of fingerprints, and will have supervisory or disciplinary duties over minors.
- Other fields where criminal background checks are required are education, health care and security. Fingerprinting and criminal history background checks are required, but employers may not seek information about an applicant's arrests that did not result in conviction.
- Telephone corporations must perform background checks on applicants for employment.
- Fingerprinting is required in California of those whose contact with community care facility clients and children in day care facilities may pose a risk to the health and safety of the clients or children.
- Fingerprints may also be requested from an applicant for employment or from a director, officer or employee of a bank, holding company or bank subsidiary for purposes of discovering the existence and nature of any criminal records, but only with the consent of the person affected.

SEARCHES AVAILABLE

- County Court Searches
- Sexual Offender
- Incarceration Records
- State records* (fingerprinting & entity must be pre-approved and job class authorized by state law)
- Workers' Compensation Records* (with pre-approval by the state WCAB)

Colorado

Colorado Rev. Stat. §§ 2472308 (IIfI); 83108(m)

- Employers may not inquire about arrest for civil or military disobedience unless it resulted in conviction.
- May not be required to disclose any information in a sealed record; may answer questions about arrests or convictions as though they had not occurred.

- Agency guidelines for pre-employment inquiries: Colorado Civil Rights Division, Publications, "Preventing Job Discrimination" found at http://www.dora.state.co.us/civil-rights/Publications.htm
- Special laws exist for employment for nonpublic schools, education boards, public school districts, nurses aides, child care centers, nursing care facilities and emergency medical technicians. Special rules apply to the employment of persons convicted of offenses involving moral turpitude.
- Nursing care facilities or persons seeking employment at a nursing care facility are authorized to obtain the required criminal background check on the applicant through the state bureau of investigation or through a state-authorized private enterprise that provides criminal background checks. In either case, a criminal background check must be conducted not more than 90 days prior to an applicant's employment.

Colorado Rev. Stat. 12.14.3.101.12.14.3.109 12.14.3 15.3
Colorado Rev. Stat. 12.14.3 103(1) (c) (11)
   1. Definitions §12-14.3-102
   2. Permissible Purpose: §12-14.3-103
   3. Accuracy §12-14.3-103.5. Consumer reports—accuracy of information
Whenever a consumer reporting agency prepares a consumer report, the agency shall follow reasonable procedures to assure maximum possible accuracy of the information concerning the consumer about whom the report relates
   4. Charges §12-14.3-105
   5. Reporting of information prohibited §12-14.3-105.3
   6. Procedure for disputed information §12-14.3-106

§27-1-110 "Conviction" means a verdict of guilty by a judge or jury or a plea of guilty or nolo contendere that is accepted by the court or adjudication for an offense that would constitute a criminal offense if committed by an adult. "Conviction" also includes having received a deferred judgment and sentence or deferred adjudication; except that a person shall not be deemed to have been convicted if the person has successfully completed a deferred sentence or deferred adjudication.

See also:
§ 12-38-108. Regarding Nursing
§ 16-22-110. Colorado sex offender registry—creation—maintenance—release of information
§ 22-1-121. Nonpublic schools—employment of personnel—notification by department of education
§ 22-32-109.8. Applicants selected for nonlicensed positions—submittal of form and fingerprints—prohibition against employing persons failing to comply
§ 25-1-124.5. Nursing care facilities—employees—criminal history check

SEARCHES AVAILABLE
- County Court Searches
- Sexual Offender
- Incarceration Records
- State Repository

Connecticut

Connecticut General Stat. §§ 46a79 to 7980; 3151i
- State policy encourages hiring qualified applicants with criminal records. If an employment application form contains any question concerning criminal history, it must include the following notice in clear and conspicuous language: "The applicant is not required to disclose the existence of any arrest, criminal charge or conviction, the records of which have been erased." Employer may not disclose information about a job applicant's criminal history to anyone except members of the personnel department. (If there is no personnel department, then only to person[s] in charge of hiring or conducting the interview.)

Connecticut Public Act No. 02-136 and specifically Section 31-51i of the general statutes
- May not be asked to disclose information about a criminal record that has been erased; may answer any question as though arrest or conviction never took place. Applicants may not be discriminated against in hiring or continued employment on the basis of an erased criminal record.

Title 36a. The Banking Law of Connecticut chapter 669. Regulated Activities part V. Consumer Credit Reports
- Credit report not initiated by consumer
- Definitions

SEARCHES AVAILABLE
- County Court Searches
- Sexual Offender
- Incarceration Records
- State Repository
- Workers' Compensation Records

Delaware

Delaware Code tit. 11, § 4374(e) along with others
- Do not have to disclose an arrest record that has been expunged.
- Title 11. Crimes and Criminal Procedure, Part V. Law-Enforcement Administration Chapter 85. State Bureau Of Identification

- Criminal background check laws cover employment in public schools, child care facilities, health facilities, home health agencies, nursing homes, security guards, private investigators, ambulance attendants, emergency medical technicians, paramedics, and correction employees.
- No employer that operates a health care facility or child care facility may hire a job applicant without requesting and receiving a Child Abuse Registry check and an Adult Abuse Registry check on that person. A signed statement must be obtained from a job applicant authorizing a full release of information provided by the Child Abuse Registry and the Adult Abuse Registry. If circumstances warrant, a person may be hired conditionally after the employer requests a Child Abuse Registry check and Adult Abuse Registry check but before the results of the checks are received. Violators are subject to a civil penalty of not less than $1,000 or more than $5,000 for each violation.
- No employer that operates a nursing home or a home health agency or a management company or other entity that contracts to operate a nursing home or a home health agency may hire an applicant without obtaining a report of the person's entire criminal history record from the State Bureau of Identification and a report from the Department of Health and Social Services regarding its review of a report of the person's entire federal criminal history.
- § 1142 Mandatory drug testing.
  (a) No employer who operates a nursing home, management company, other business entity contracted to operate a nursing home, or agency that refers employees to work in a nursing home may hire any applicant, as defined in § 1141 of this title, without first obtaining the results of such applicant's mandatory drug screening.

SEARCHES AVAILABLE

- County Court Searches
- Sexual Offender
- Incarceration Records
- State Repository* (signed release)

District of Columbia

D.C. Code § 21402.66 along with others
- Employers may not obtain or inquire into arrest record.
- Convictions. May obtain record of convictions occurring within the last 10 years.
§ 44-552. Criminal background checks

SEARCHES AVAILABLE

- County Court Searches
- Sexual Offender

- Incarceration Records
- State Repository* (notarized release)

Florida

Florida. Stat. § 112.011 along with others
- May not be disqualified to practice or pursue any occupation or profession that requires a license, permit or certificate because of a prior conviction, unless it was for a felony or first degree misdemeanor and is directly related to the specific line of work.
- Anyone who has had a criminal record sealed may lawfully deny the events covered by the sealed record, except when the person applies for a job with a criminal justice agency or seeks a license or employment working in a safety sensitive position under the auspices of the state health and human services agency or as a licensed teacher or child care worker.
- Criminal background check laws cover employment for school district employees, substitute teachers, service provider personnel who have direct contact with unmarried minor and developmentally disabled clients, crisis stabilization units, residential treatment facilities, residential treatment centers for children and adolescents, birth centers, abortion clinics, hospitals, ambulatory surgical centers, mobile surgical facilities and private utilization review agents, nursing homes, home health agencies, nurse registries, adult day care centers, hospices, clinical labs, multiphasic health testing centers, fire safety inspectors and firefighters, law enforcement and corrections officers, financial institutions, public officers and employees who hold positions of special trust or sensitive location and seaport employees.
- The Florida Department of Law Enforcement may require fingerprinting for criminal background investigations of state lottery vendors, retailers and employees.
- The salaried staff and volunteers of nonprofit centers that make after school hours for children more productive may be required to submit fingerprints for background checks as a condition of employment.
- Upon employment, noninstructional personnel hired to fill positions requiring direct contact with students in any district school system must file a set of fingerprints with a law enforcement officer or district person authorized to take fingerprints. The employee is on probation until a criminal background check is completed. Fingerprinting is required as part of the certification process for teachers and substitute teachers.
- State agencies must designate the positions that they consider sensitive enough to require a background check that includes fingerprinting as a condition of employment.
- Alcohol and drug treatment resource personnel must submit a set of fingerprints for a criminal background check within five days after starting work.

- Fire safety inspectors, fire fighters, law enforcement, correctional officers and probation officers must submit fingerprints for criminal background checks.

SEARCHES AVAILABLE
- County Court Searches
- Sexual Offender
- Incarceration Records
- State Repository
- Workers' Compensation Records

Georgia

Georgia Code §§ 35334; 42862 to 42863 along with others
- In order to obtain a criminal record from the state Crime Information Center, employer must supply the individual's fingerprints or signed consent. If an adverse employment decision is made on the basis of the record, must disclose all information in the record to the employee or applicant and tell how it affected the decision.
- Probation for a first offense is not a conviction; may not be disqualified for employment once probation is completed.
- Employees of private detective and security agency license holders in Georgia must be fingerprinted.
- Before an applicant may become an employee of any daycare facility, a record check application—including fingerprinting—must be submitted.
- Before an applicant may become an employee of any nursing home, a criminal record check must be requested from the Georgia Crime Information Center. A nursing home must not employ a person with an unsatisfactory determination.
- Accompanying any application for a new license for a personal care home where residents reside, the applicant must furnish to the Department of Human Resources a record check application for the director and each employee of the facility.
- Employers may require that new or current employees who supervise children submit to a criminal records check.

Title 10. Commerce And Trade
Chapter 1. Selling And Other Trade Practices, Article 15. Deceptive Or Unfair Practices, Part 2. Fair Business Practices Act
10-1-392 Definitions; when intentional violation occurs.
    1. Definitions
    2. Adverse Action
Also: Georgia Code §50.701 §50.722 §50.704

- County Court Searches
- Sexual Offender
- Incarceration Records
- State Repository* (fingerprints required)

Hawaii

Hawaii Rev. Stat. §§ 3782.to 3782.5; 8313.2 along with others
- It is a violation of law for any employer to refuse to hire, to discharge or to discriminate in terms of compensation, conditions or privileges of employment because of a person's arrest or court record.
- Employers may inquire about and consider an individual's criminal conviction record in the process of making a decision about hiring. The investigation may go back 10 years, but may only be made after a conditional job offer has been extended. If a conviction record bears a rational relationship to the duties and responsibilities of the position, the conditional job offer may be withdrawn. The criminal conviction (not arrest) records, going back 10 years, of current employees may be checked when making a decision about termination or the terms, conditions or privileges of employment, if a conviction bears a rational relationship to the duties and responsibilities of the position.
- Employers cannot consider misdemeanor convictions for which a jail sentence cannot be imposed.
- Criminal background check laws exist for employment for public and private schools, adult foster and developmental disabilities homes, child care facilities and institutions, youth correctional facilities, correctional facilities and the insurance business.
- Staff members and prospective staff members of correctional institutions in Hawaii must undergo criminal history record checks. They must submit a statement under penalty of perjury indicating whether they have ever been convicted of a crime, other than a minor traffic violation, consent to a records check and be fingerprinted. Youth correctional facility staff members and new staff members must be fingerprinted within five working days.
- A person may not provide or be hired to provide armed security services at airports without consenting to a criminal history records check, including a fingerprint check.
- The department of education and private schools may consider criminal convictions in determining whether a prospective employee is suited to working in close proximity to children. Employees and applicants for certain education positions are required to undergo fingerprinting and a criminal history record check. Similarly, hospitals, nursing homes, home health agencies, and other health care

facilities are permitted to consider criminal records in determining whether or not an employee or prospective employee is properly suited to working in close proximity to vulnerable patients.
- Applicants to operate a child care facility and their prospective employees must submit fingerprints.
- If an arrest or conviction has been expunged, may state that no record exists and may respond to questions as a person with no record would respond.
- Agency guidelines for pre-employment inquiries: Hawaii Civil Rights Commission, "Guide to Pre-Employment Inquiries" found at http://www.state.hi.us/hcrc/brochures.html

SEARCHES AVAILABLE
- County Court Searches
- Incarceration Records
- State Repository
- Workers' Compensation Records

Idaho

- Agency guidelines for pre-employment inquiries: Idaho Human Rights Commission, "Pre-Employment Inquiries" researched through http://www.humanrightsidaho.org/links.html
- Background check laws have been established for employment for school district personnel, child care centers, personal care centers, healthcare providers and lottery workers.
- Each school district may require all persons hired for the first time or who have been in the employ of the district for five years or less to undergo a criminal history check. Persons who have been convicted of a felony will be subject to immediate termination or other action. Persons employed for more than five years may be required to undergo criminal history checks.
- The securities act registration requirements for broker-dealers, salespersons and investment advisors include the submission of fingerprints, unless waived, to the Director of Finance.

SEARCHES AVAILABLE
- County Court Searches
- Sexual Offender
- Incarceration Records
- State Repository
- Workers' Compensation Records

Illinois

775 Illinois Comp. Stat. § 5/2103 along with others
- It is a civil rights violation to ask about an arrest or criminal history record that has been expunged or sealed, or to use the fact of an arrest or criminal history record as a basis for refusing to hire or to renew employment. Law does not prohibit employer from using other means to find out if person actually engaged in conduct for which they were arrested.
- State agencies, local governmental units and school districts and private organizations may utilize conviction information obtained from the Department of State Police in evaluating the qualifications and character of an employee or prospective employee.
- Applicants for jobs in facilities run by the Department of Mental Health and Developmental Disabilities must submit to criminal background checks, based on their fingerprints. Applicants may be hired conditionally, pending the results of the background check, but must be notified that employment is dependent on the results of the check. Applicants who decline to submit to testing may be rejected.
- Persons applying for medical licenses must undergo criminal history background checks.
- Fingerprints are required for every police officer and fire fighter to be sent to the FBI. Prior to appointment, fingerprints are required from all auxiliary police, sheriffs and state police.
- Application for permanent employee registration cards requires fingerprints from all private alarm contractor, detective agency and security agency employees.
- The Health Care Worker Background Check Act applies to all individuals employed or retained by a health care employer as home health care aides, nurse aides, personal care assistants, private duty nurse aides, day training personnel, or an individual working in any similar health-related occupation where he or she provides direct care.
- Before hiring an employee or independent contractor to perform work involving facilities used for the distribution of natural gas to customers, a public utility must require a completed certificate listing the proposed employee's or independent contractor's violations of pertinent safety or environmental laws.

SEARCHES AVAILABLE
- County Court Searches
- Sexual Offender
- Incarceration Records
- State Repository
- Workers' Compensation Records

Indiana

- IC 35-38-5-5 Limited criminal history records may not be disclosed if are over 15 years old if the subject petitioned to limit access to their limited criminal history.
- Background checks for employment are required for child care facilities, child care ministries, home health care agencies, nurse aides, unlicensed employees of health care facilities, and private detectives and their personnel.
- Home health care agencies are prohibited from employing anyone to provide services in a patient's or client's temporary or permanent residence if that person's limited criminal history indicates that the person has been convicted of rape, criminal deviate conduct, exploitation of an endangered adult, failure to report battery, neglect or exploitation of an endangered adult or theft, if the conviction for theft occurred less than 10 years before the person's application date.
- A home health agency may not employ a person to provide services in a patient's or client's temporary or permanent residence for more than three calendar days without receipt of that person's limited criminal history, unless the Indiana central repository for criminal history information is solely responsible for failing to provide the person's limited criminal history to the home health agency within the required time.
- Limited criminal history information may be used in determining whether to grant or deny a teaching license.
- Private detective licensees in Indiana must furnish their employees with identification cards containing the employee's thumb print. In addition, the licensee must maintain a full set of each employee's fingerprints (both hands) on file and file a duplicate set with the Indiana State Police.

SEARCHES AVAILABLE
- County Court Searches
- Sexual Offender
- Incarceration Records
- State Repository

Iowa

- Agency guidelines for pre-employment inquiries: Iowa Civil Rights Commission, "Successfully Interviewing Job Applicants" found at: http://www.state.ia.us/government/crc/successfullyinquiries.html
- The criminal records check employment laws pertain to the employment of personnel in child care and dependent adult care facilities. Prior to employment of a person in a facility, the facility must request that the department of public safety perform criminal and dependent adult abuse, and child abuse record checks of the person. This requirement applies to home care, hospices, assisted living facilities, and elder group homes.

SEARCHES AVAILABLE
- County Court Searches
- Sexual Offender
- Incarceration Records
- State Repository
- Workers' Compensation Records

Kansas

Kansas Stat. §§ 124516(g); 214619(h); 224710 along with others
- Employers can not inspect or inquire into criminal record unless employee or applicant signs a release.
- If arrest, conviction or diversion record is expunged, do not have to disclose any information about it.
- Special situations: Employers are entitled to obtain complete criminal record information for brokers or investment advisors, commercial drivers and sensitive positions in the state lottery, state gaming agency or pari-mutuel racing.
- The state has criminal background check laws for employment for adult care homes and home health care agencies.
- Individuals are prohibited from operating an adult care home if they employ any person who has a criminal history background. However, individuals may be hired on a conditional basis pending the outcome of a criminal background check. No person who has been employed by the same adult care home for five consecutive years immediately prior to July 1, 1998, is subject to the background check requirement, while employed by the same adult care home. Individuals who have been the subject of a criminal background check within one year prior to applying for employment in an adult care home are exempt from the background check requirement.
- Employers may ask prospective independent contractors to sign releases of their criminal records. The employer remains liable for any employment decisions based on the criminal records.
- Agency guidelines for pre-employment inquiries: Kansas Human Rights Commission, "Guidelines on Equal Employment Practices: Preventing Discrimination in Hiring" found at http://www.khrc.net/hiring.html

KANSAS STATUTES
Chapter 50.—Unfair Trade And Consumer Protection Article 7—Fair Credit Reporting
See: 701,722, 704
Kansas Statute Section 50.714
1. Definitions §50-702
2. Permissible purpose: §50-703
3. Obsolete information - what can be reported §50-704
4. Disclosure §50-705, §50-708

5. Compliance §50-706
6. Disputes of accuracy §50-710
7. Charges §50-711
8. Public record information for employment §50-712
9. Restrictions §50-713
10. Requirements on users §50-714

SEARCHES AVAILABLE

- County Court Searches
- Sexual Offender
- Incarceration Records
- State Repository
- Workers' Compensation Records

Kentucky

- Various law sections provide definitions and certain code sections relate to child care, teachers, and others.
- Individuals who provide direct services to senior citizens may not have a criminal history. In addition, employees with felony convictions related to theft, abuse or sale of illegal drugs, abuse or neglect of an adult, or the commission of a sex crime may not be employed by state-funded social service agencies or nursing facilities in jobs involving personal or group interaction between the employee and a senior citizen.
- Applications for employment for these positions must prominently state: FOR THIS TYPE OF EMPLOYMENT STATE LAW REQUIRES A CRIMINAL RECORD CHECK AS A CONDITION OF EMPLOYMENT. Criminal records must also be obtained for individuals seeking employment in nursing facilities that do not cater specifically to senior citizens.
- An employer may request from the Justice Cabinet or the Administrative Office of the Courts the criminal records of any person who applies for employment or volunteers for a position that would involve supervisory or disciplinary power over a minor. Requested information includes all available convictions involving any (1) felony or misdemeanor sexual offense or offense involving pornography; or (2) misdemeanor committed within the five years immediately preceding the application involving controlled substances or DUI conviction.
- Child care centers may not employ any person who is a violent offender or has been convicted of a sex crime in a position that involves supervisory or disciplinary power or direct contact over a minor.
- School superintendents must require a national and state criminal background check, including a fingerprint check, on all newly certified hires. Individuals who were employed in another certified position in a Kentucky school district within

six months of the date of hire, and who had previously submitted to a national and state criminal background check for the previous employment are exempt from the background check requirement. If a vacancy occurs during a school term, a super-intendent may employ an individual who will have supervisory or disciplinary authority over minors on a probationary basis, pending receipt of the criminal history background check. Superintendents may not employ individuals who are violent offenders or who have been convicted of a sex crime. However, a superintendent may employ, at the superintendent's discretion, persons convicted of sex crimes classified as misdemeanors.

See: KRS §17.10(1) Employers' ability to request criminal records where the position would have supervisory or disciplinary power over a minor.

SEARCHES AVAILABLE
- County Court Searches
- Sexual Offender
- Incarceration Records
- State Repository
- Workers' Compensation Records

Louisiana

Louisiana Rev. Stat. § 37:2950 along with others
- Prior conviction cannot be used as a basis to deny employment or an occupational or professional license, unless conviction is for a felony and directly relates to the job or license being sought.
- Special situations: Protection does not apply to law enforcement, various state boards, state racing, medical, engineering and architecture or funeral and embalming licenses.
- If the results of a criminal history background check reveal that any licensed ambulance personnel or non-licensed person has been convicted of an offense that includes the distribution or possession with the intent to distribute controlled substances, the employer may refuse to hire or contract with that person.
- It is unlawful for a public or private employer to recover the costs of fingerprinting that is required as a condition of employment from applicants or employees.
- No person may be hired by the state department of health and human services to investigate child abuse or to work in a juvenile detention center, correction or treatment facility until a set of the individual's fingerprints has been submitted.

Louisiana Rev. Stat. 357.1
1. Access to files/information
2. Definitions

SEARCHES AVAILABLE
- County Court Searches
- Sexual Offender
- Incarceration Records
- Workers' Compensation Records

Maine

Me. Rev. Stat. tit. 5, § 5301; tit. 28A, § 703A; Code Me. R. 94348 Ch. 3, § 3.06(B7) along with others
- No one can be denied employment because of refusing to answer a pre-employment inquiry that is unlawful under the Maine Human Rights Act or Maine Human Rights Commission Rules. A conviction is not an automatic bar to obtaining an occupational or professional license; only convictions that directly relate to the profession or occupation; that include dishonesty or false statements; that are subject to imprisonment for more than one year; or involve sexual misconduct on the part of a licensee may be considered.
- Special situations: Liquor retailers may not employ anyone convicted of selling liquor to minors or selling liquor without a license within the past two years (for a first offense), or within the past five years (for a second offense).
- Prior to issuing a teaching certificate, authorization, approval or renewal, all state educational personnel are required to undergo a state and federal criminal history record check that includes submitting two fingerprint cards. In making a decision regarding suitability for licensing, the commissioner may rely on information provided by the Federal Bureau of Investigation that was taken within the 24-month period prior to a request for criminal history information. All information obtained from a criminal record check is confidential. The expense of the criminal record check must be paid by the applicant.
- If necessary to resolve any question of identity, fingerprints may be required of employees of security guard firms to the Maine Commissioner of Public Safety.

Agency guidelines for pre-employment inquiries: Maine Human Rights Commission, Publications, "Pre-Employment Inquiry Guidelines" found at http://www.state.me.us/mhrc/publish.htm

MAINE REVISED STATUTES
Title 10. Commerce And Trade, Part 3. Regulation Of Trade, Chapter 210. Fair Credit Reporting Act

Maine Rev. Stat. tit. 10.1311.1329
Maine Rev. Stat. tit. 10.1314.2 A

Maine Rev. Stat. tit. 10.1314.1 A
Maine Rev. Stat. tit. 10.1314.2.B & C.
Maine Rev. Stat. tit.10. 1319.2
1316 and 1317 Maine Act
Maine Rev. Stat. tit. 10. 1320
Maine Rev. Stat. tit. 10. 1320.3
Maine Fair Credit Reporting Act 10 M.R.S.A. §1313-1314 to 1321 & 1323 & 1326
  1. Definitions
  2. Permissible Purposes of Credit Reports § 1313-A
  3. Reporting of information
  4. Disclosure
  5. Notices
  6. Correcting inaccuracies
  7. Public Record - Adverse action
  8. Accuracy of information

SEARCHES AVAILABLE

- County Court Searches
- Sexual Offender
- Incarceration Records
- State Repository

Maryland

Md. Code [Crim. Proc.], § 10109; Md. Regs. Code 09.01.10.02 along with others
- Employers may not inquire about any criminal charges that have been expunged. May not use a refusal to disclose information as basis for not hiring an applicant.
- Need not refer to nor give any information about an expunged charge. A professional or occupational license may not be refused or revoked simply because of a conviction; agency must consider the nature of the crime and its relation to the occupation or profession; the conviction's relevance to the applicant's fitness and qualifications; when conviction occurred and other convictions, if any; and the applicant's behavior before and after conviction.
- Before an eligible employee may begin work for an adult dependent care program, the program must apply for a state criminal history records check or request a private agency to conduct a background check. As part of the check, eligible employees must submit a complete set of legible fingerprints. The adult dependent care program may also require an alcohol or controlled dangerous substance test.
- Before the first day of employment or the first day of actual operation of the facility, employers and employees of the following facilities must apply for state and federal criminal background checks, including a complete set of fingerprints: child

care centers, homes and institutions; family care centers; juvenile detention, correction or treatment facilities; public and certain private schools; foster care home or group facilities; and recreation centers for minors.

CODE OF MARYLAND - COMMERCIAL LAW
Title 14. Miscellaneous Consumer Protection Provisions, Subtitle 12—Consumer Credit Reporting Agencies

Maryland Code Com. Law 14.1201.14.1218. 14-1203
Maryland Code Com Law 14. 1201(1) (2) (1)
Maryland Code Commercial Law Sec. 14.1212(a)
1. Definitions
2. Permissible purpose § 14-1202
3. Information excluded
4. Disclosure
5. Agency procedures
6. Disputes over accuracy
7. Fees
8. Disclosure of public record
9. Adverse action
10. Notification
11. Statements to consumers

SEARCHES AVAILABLE
- County Court Searches
- Sexual Offender
- Incarceration Records
- State Repository
- Workers' Compensation Records

Massachusetts

Mass. Gen. Laws ch. 151B, § 4; ch. 276, § 100A; Mass. Regs. Code tit. 804, § 3.02 along with others
- If job application has a question about prior arrests or convictions, it must state that an applicant with a sealed record is entitled to answer, "No record."
- Arrest records. May not ask about arrests that did not result in conviction.
- Convictions. May obtain record of convictions occurring within the last 10 years. May not ask about first-time convictions for drunkenness, simple assault, speeding, minor traffic violations or disturbing the peace.
- May not inquire about misdemeanor convictions where the date of the conviction

or the completion of incarceration, whichever date is later, occurred five or more years prior to the date of application for employment, unless the conviction was within the five years immediately preceding the date of the application for employment.
- If criminal record is sealed, may answer, "No record," to any inquiry about past arrests or convictions.
- Agencies that provide home health aides, companions and certain other types of services to the elderly or to persons with disabilities and long-term care facilities must obtain all available criminal record information on individuals who will provide services before the individuals may be employed.
- The school committee, superintendent and principal of any public school will have access to criminal offender record information regarding all applicants for all school positions, including subcontractors and laborers who perform work on school grounds if there may be direct contact between the applicant and school children.
- Operators of camps for children and any entities or organizations primarily engaged in providing activities or programs to children 18 years or under that accept volunteers must obtain all available criminal offender record information for prospective and present employees and volunteers. This information should be used only for the purpose of furthering the protection of children.

MASSACHUSETTS GENERAL LAWS
Part I. Administration Of The Government, Title Xv. Regulation Of Trade, Chapter 93. Regulation Of Trade And Certain Enterprises, Consumer Credit Reporting

Massachusetts Gen Laws ch.93.50.68 93.52
Massachusetts Gen Laws ch.93.50
Massachusetts Gen Laws ch.93.53
1. Definitions
2. Permissible purpose § 51
3. Information in reports
4. Disclosure
5. Procedures by CRA's
6. Disclosure—for credit..." " statement to be included with disclosure
7. Accuracy
8. Charges
9. Notices for public records
10. Procedures for accurate reporting
11. Adverse action
12. Denial of credit or employment = " " Statement made § 62
13. Prohibited information

SEARCHES AVAILABLE
- County Court Searches
- Sexual Offender
- Incarceration Records
- State Repository
- Workers' Compensation Records

Michigan

Michigan Comp. Laws § 37.2205a along with others
- Employers may not request information on any arrests or misdemeanor charges that did not result in conviction.
- Employees or applicants are not making a false statement if they fail to disclose information they have a civil right to withhold.
- If a person is convicted of not more than one offense, they may file an application with that jurisdiction to set the conviction aside. If the order is granted, the record becomes "non-public" except where application is for law enforcement. MCLA 780.623
- Agency guidelines for pre-employment inquiries: Michigan Civil Rights Commission, "Pre-Employment Inquiry Guide" found at: http://www.michigan.gov/documents/pre-employment_inquery_guide_13019_7.pdf
- The backgrounds of health professionals may be investigated before being granted licenses. Licensing will be denied if statutorily-specified convictions are discovered.
- Private security guard licensees must take fingerprints of their employees and prospective employees—employees may be employed temporarily pending processing and approval.
- Unless the requirement is waived, all persons employed by a broker-dealer, commodity issuer or investment advisor who are regularly employed must be fingerprinted as a condition of employment.
- It is unlawful to compel newly hired employees or employees returning from leave to pay the cost of fingerprinting.
- It is a crime for a person to obtain or attempt to obtain another person's personal identity information with the intent of unlawfully using the information to obtain employment without the person's authorization.
- A school receiving an application from a person for the position of school bus driver or pupil transportation vehicle driver must request from the Michigan Department of State Police a background check to determine whether the person was convicted of criminal sexual conduct or felonious assault on a child, child abuse, or cruelty, torture or indecent exposure involving a child.
- An individual currently or prospectively employed or volunteering at a child care

center, child caring institution or child placing agency, may upon written request receive documentation from the Michigan Department of Social Services stating that the individual is not named in a central registry case as the perpetrator of child abuse or child neglect.
- Operators of child care centers or child caring institutions are required to conspicuously post on the premises a notice whether that child care center or institution requires a criminal history check on its employees or volunteers.

SEARCHES AVAILABLE
- County Court Searches
- Sexual Offender
- Incarceration Records
- State Repository
- Workers' Compensation Records

Minnesota

Minnesota Stat. §§ 364.01 to 364.03 along with others
- State policy encourages the rehabilitation of criminal offenders; employment opportunity is considered essential to rehabilitation.
- No one can be disqualified from pursuing or practicing an occupation that requires a license, unless the crime directly relates to the occupation. Agency may consider the nature and seriousness of the crime and its relation to the applicant's fitness for the occupation. Even if the crime does relate to the occupation, a person who provides evidence of rehabilitation and present fitness cannot be disqualified.
- Employers cannot consider misdemeanor convictions for which a jail sentence cannot be imposed.
- Records may be sealed for first time drug offenders and become non-public. MSA §609A.02
- Agency guidelines for pre-employment inquiries: Minnesota Department of Human Rights, "Hiring, Job Interviews and the Minnesota Human Rights Act" found at http://www.humanrights.state.mn.us/employer_hiring.html
- School hiring authorities must require criminal background checks on all persons who are offered employment in their schools. If a background check was performed by another school within the past 12 months, the results are on file with the other school or otherwise easily accessible, the applicant gives written permission to use the earlier background check results and there is no reason to believe the applicant has committed a disqualifying act since the background check was made, a school may use the earlier record check.
- Criminal background checks are not required for persons who are hold initial entrance licenses issued within the previous 12 months by the state board of teaching or education.

- Schools are permitted to run checks on volunteers, independent contractors and student employees. If a school district elects to require background checks, an individual may not be on school grounds without providing a signed consent form and the fee for the check.
- When employment is offered to out-of-state residents, school districts must request background checks from both the Minnesota Bureau of Criminal Apprehension and the parallel agency in the other state, or the FBI if the other state does not have an instate agency. The individual must provide a consent form and pay the background check fee.

Minnesota Stat. §13C.001.13C.04
Minnesota Statute Section §13C.02 subdivision 1
Minnesota Statute Section §13C.03
  1. Permissible purpose §13C001. Subd. 3
  2. Definitions
  3. Fees
  4. Disclosure
  5. Adverse action
  6. Notice

SEARCHES AVAILABLE

- County Court Searches
- Sexual Offender
- Incarceration Records
- State Repository
- Workers' Compensation Records

Mississippi

Title 37 relates to Education.
MS ST §§99

- By completing all requirements, a person not formally charged or prosecuted or upon dismissal of the charge, for any misdemeanor, may have the matter expunged.
- A first time offender for a misdemeanor may petition the court to expunge the record.
- Prospective employees of residential institutions, facilities, clinics, organizations and other entities that provide children with services, including care, lodging, maintenance, counseling or therapy for alcohol or controlled substance abuse, or any other emotional disorder or mental illness are required to follow a pre-employment procedure that includes a national criminal history background check and fingerprint check.

- No child residential facility may employ any person, or allow any person to serve as a volunteer, who would provide services to children for the entity if the person:
  - Has a felony conviction for a crime against persons;
  - Has a felony conviction under the Uniform Controlled Substances Act;
  - Has a conviction for a crime of child abuse or neglect;
  - Has a conviction for any sex offense; or
  - Has a conviction for any other offense committed in another jurisdiction or any federal offense that would constitute one of the offenses listed above without regard to its designation in that jurisdiction or under federal law.
- Any child residential facility that fails to complete sex offense criminal history record information and felony conviction record information checks as described above will be subject to a penalty of up to $10,000 for each such violation and may be enjoined from further operation until it complies.
- The Mississippi tax commission is authorized to require fingerprinting of an applicant or licensee, and the casino and alcoholic beverage personnel of a licensee, and the forwarding of all fingerprints taken to the FBI.

SEARCHES AVAILABLE

- County Court Searches
- Sexual Offender
- Mississippi
- Incarceration Records

Missouri

- Agency guidelines for pre-employment inquiries: Commission on Human Rights, Missouri Department of Labor and Industrial Relations, "Pre-Employment Inquiries" found at: http://www.dolir.state.mo.us/hr/interview.htm
- Criminal background checks are required for health care and educational professionals and applicants for positions as health care and educational professionals.
- Child care, elder care and personal care workers must complete a registration form for the state's family care safety registry provided by the Department of Health within 15 days of the beginning of their employment. Failure to submit the form without good cause is a class B misdemeanor.

SEARCHES AVAILABLE

- County Court Searches
- Incarceration Records
- State Repository

Montana

MONTANA CODE
Title 31. Credit Transactions And Relationships, Chapter 3. Related Credit Practices,
Part 1. Consumer Reporting Agencies
Montana Code Sections 31.3.101.31.3.153 31.3.112, 31.3.131

      1. Permissible purpose § 31-3-111
      2. Definitions § 31-3-102
      3. Obsolete information § 31-3-112
      4. Disclosure § 31-3-113
      5. Compliance procedures § 31-3-114
      6. Adverse information § 31-3-115
      7. Disclosures § 31-3-122
      8. Disputes § 31-3-124
      9. Public record information for employment purposes § 31-3-126
     10. Requirements on users § 31-3-131

- Upon completion of a deferred sentence, the court may allow the defendant to withdraw a plea of guilty or no contest, or may strike the verdict of guilty from the record and order that the charge or charges be dismissed. Once dismissed, the records may only be obtained upon a showing of good cause. MCA 46-18-204.
- Criminal records checks are required for employment in facilities caring for the elderly and the developmentally disabled and for teachers before being hired to work in schools.
- Applicants for licensing as security companies, security guards, and private investigators must submit evidence under oath of not being convicted of certain crimes, not suffering from habitual drunkenness or drug dependence and of being of good moral character. The license application must also include two sets of fingerprints.

SEARCHES AVAILABLE

- County Court Searches
- Sexual Offender
- Incarceration Records
- State Repository
- Workers' Compensation Records

Nebraska

Nebraska Rev. Stat. § 293523 along with others
- Employers may not obtain access to information regarding arrests that do not lead to conviction.
- Duty of CRA

- Everyone who works with persons with developmental disabilities and does not hold a professional license must undergo a criminal background record check. The requirement covers persons who work for either state-operated services or private businesses that contract with the state. Individuals must file a complete set of fingerprints with the state patrol. The state patrol will make its own search and transmit the fingerprints to the FBI for a national check.

SEARCHES AVAILABLE
- County Court Searches
- Sexual Offender
- Incarceration Records
- State Repository
- Workers' Compensation Records

Nevada

Nevada Rev. Stat. § 179A.100(3) along with others
- Employers may obtain a prospective employee's criminal history record only if it includes convictions or a pending charge, including parole or probation.
- Agency guidelines for pre-employment inquiries: Nevada Equal Rights Commission, "Pre-Employment Inquiry Guide" found at http://detr.state.nv.us/nerc/nerc_preemp.htm
- Every applicant for a teaching license or a license to perform other educational functions must submit with the application a complete set of fingerprints and written permission to authorize the school superintendent to forward the fingerprints to the Federal Bureau of Investigation and to the central repository for Nevada records of criminal history for their reports on the criminal history of the applicant. As part of a criminal background check, a Nevada school district may require fingerprinting and written permission to forward them to the Federal Bureau of Investigation (FBI) from teachers' aides and other auxiliary nonprofessional personnel who assist teachers in instructing children.
- Every employee or prospective employee of a foster home or child care facility licensee and every adult resident therein must submit a set of fingerprints and written authorization to forward them to the FBI for a criminal background check.
- Certain personnel of labor organizations that represent gaming industry employees must file their fingerprints for a background check.
- Applicants for security guard work cards may be required by a county sheriff to submit their fingerprints for a criminal background check by the FBI.

Nevada Rev. Stat. 589C.010.598C200. 598C.152
Nevada Rev. Stat. 589C.060.
1. Definitions
2. Permissible Purposes FCRA 1681

3. Duties
4. Disclosure
5. Adverse Action
6. Files
7. Remedies

SEARCHES AVAILABLE
- County Court Searches
- Sexual Offender
- Incarceration Records
- State Repository* (fingerprints required)

New Hampshire

New Hampshire Rev. Stat. § 651:5 (Xc); N.H. Code Admin. R. Hum 405.03 along with others
- Employers may ask about a previous criminal record only if question substantially follows this wording, "Have you ever been arrested for or convicted of a crime that has not been annulled by a court?"
- Arrest records. It is unlawful discrimination for an employer to ask about an arrest record, to have a job requirement that applicant have no arrest record or to use information about arrest record to make a hiring decision, unless it is a business necessity. It is unlawful discrimination to ask about arrest record if it has the purpose or effect of discouraging applicants of a particular racial or national origin group.
- Prospective employees with school administrative units, school districts, or charter schools are subject to a state and national criminal records check. A prospective employee will not be eligible for employment if found to be convicted of (1) murder; (2) child pornography; (3) aggravated felonious sexual assault; (4) felonious sexual assault; or (5) kidnapping. The criminal background check requirement also applies to private businesses and agencies that contract with school administrative units, school districts or charter schools to provide services where the contractor or employees of the contractor would have direct contact with student (i.e. cafeteria workers, school bus drivers, or custodial personnel).
- Child day care providers who are required to be licensed must submit to the Department of Health and Human Services, within 30 days of their arrival, the names, birth names, birth dates and addresses of staff, household members, and others who will have regular contact with the children.

STATE OF NEW HAMPSHIRE , Title XXXI. Trade And Commerce, Chapter 359-B. Consumer Credit Reporting
New Hampshire Rev. Stat. 56.11.28.56.11.39; Sec. 359.B:15.1
1. Definitions
2. Permissible Purpose §359-B:4

3. Obsolete information
4. Disclosure
5. Compliance
6. Disputes
7. Fees
8. Requirements on users

SEARCHES AVAILABLE

- County Court Searches
- Sexual Offender
- Incarceration Records
- State Repository* (Authorization must be notarized)
- Workers' Compensation Records

New Jersey

New Jersey Admin. Code tit. 13, §§ 591.2, 591.6 along with others
- In order to determine work qualifications, employer may obtain criminal record information about convictions and about any pending arrests or charges. When requesting record, employer must certify in writing that he will notify applicant; will provide sufficient time for applicant to challenge, correct or complete record; and will not presume guilt for any pending charges or court actions.
- Applicants who are disqualified for employment based on criminal record must be given adequate notice and reasonable time to confirm or deny accuracy of information.
- Because crimes or disorderly person's offenses disqualify individuals from employment in state facilities for individuals with mental illnesses and for individuals with developmental disabilities, criminal record checks are required prior to employment in these positions and at least once every two years during the period of employment.
- Criminal history background checks must be conducted on all current and prospective employees in direct contact with institutionalized elderly persons. Facilities are prohibited from hiring any unlicensed person serving in a position that involves regular contact with an elderly patient. However, certain individuals may be hired on a conditional basis for no more than 180 days pending completion of a criminal history background check.
- Individuals will not be disqualified from employment on the basis of a conviction disclosed by a criminal history background check if they have affirmatively demonstrated clear and convincing evidence of rehabilitation. Individuals refusing to consent to or cooperate in the securing of a criminal history background check will not be considered for employment. The prospective employer may require the prospective employee to pay the cost of the background check.

- As a condition of obtaining or renewing a child care center license, that a criminal history background check be conducted for each staff member to determine if there are any reported incidents of child abuse or neglect involving the employees. Staff members must provide written consent for the background checks. A refusal to consent must result in immediate termination of employment. Staff members will be charged a fee for the background checks. The center may, at its discretion, offer to pay for or reimburse the staff member for the cost of the background check.
- Housing authorities are required to conduct a criminal history background check, including a fingerprint check, on all applicants seeking employment and are prohibited from employing applicants with criminal records. Individuals need not be disqualified from consideration for employment if they have shown that they are rehabilitated. Written consent is necessary for the background check and applicants who refuse to consent may not be considered for employment. The applicant is responsible for the cost of the criminal background check.
- The Department of Health and Senior Services may not issue a nurse aide or personal care assistant certification to any applicant, except on a conditional basis (with a 180-day limit), unless there is first a determination that no criminal history record information exists that would disqualify that person from being certified.
- In addition, the New Jersey Board of Nursing may not issue a homemaker-home health care aide certificate to any applicant, except on a conditional basis for 180 days, unless the board first determines that no criminal history record information exists that would disqualify that person from being certified. If a background check reveals a relevant criminal conviction, but the individual has evidence of rehabilitation, the individual will not be disqualified from certification. An applicant for certification who refuses to cooperate in securing a criminal history record check may not be issued a certificate. The employer or prospective may pay the cost of the criminal record background check or require that the employee or prospective employee bear the cost of the check.
- Public school employees must undergo criminal background record checks before being employed. Schools may hire employees provisionally while the check is being completed, but only after the school board of directors makes a special request for provisional hiring. Provisional employment generally only last for three months, however a two-month extension may be sought.
- Criminal background checks may also be required of private school employees.
- Employees and applicants for employment in the school system, including teachers, cafeteria workers, enforcement and maintenance personnel and bus drivers, who would have regular contact with students, must submit a set of fingerprints and written consent for a criminal background check.
- The Casino Control Commission has the authority to prescribe procedures for the fingerprinting of licensee employees that may be necessary for casino floor restrictions.

- Applicants for employment and current employees of mental hospitals must file a set of fingerprints and written consent with the Commissioner of Human Services for a criminal background check.
- No appointment to parking enforcement or special law enforcement positions may be made unless the applicant submits a set of fingerprints to the state and the Federal Bureau of Investigation.
- Private detective licensees must maintain one set of fingerprints of each employee and send two sets to the state within 48 hours of employment for criminal background checks.

NEW JERSEY STATUTES
Title 56. Trade Names, Trade-Marks And Unfair Trade Practices, Chapter 11. Consumer Credit Transactions
New Jersey Rev. Stat. 56:11.28 56:11.39
New Jersey Rev. Stat. 56:11 31 b(1) (a)
New Jersey Rev. Stat. 56:11 33 a (1)
1. Definitions
2. Permissible Purpose §56:11-31
3. Disclosure
4. Procedures
5. Reports to consumer
6. Time of disclosure
7. Disputes
8. Fees
9. Failure to comply

SEARCHES AVAILABLE
- County Court Searches
- Sexual Offender
- Incarceration Records
- State Repository
- Workers' Compensation Records

New Mexico

- Procedures must be in place to fingerprint applicants for teaching certification. As part of the process, applicants must provide two fingerprint cards to the department of education for an FBI background check. In addition, local school boards must develop policics and procedures to require employment background checks. The policies and procedures may include requiring applicants who have been offered employment to provide their FBI background check record.

- Certain criminal offenders may not work with children. If the offender was convicted of trafficking in controlled substances, criminal sexual penetration or related sex offenses or child abuse and has applied for reinstatement or issuance of a teaching certificate, license to operate a child-care facility or employment at a child-care facility, regardless of rehabilitation, the issuing agency may refuse to grant or renew, may suspend or revoke the offender's certification, license or employment application.
- All fire fighter applicants in municipalities with a population of 100,000 must submit a set of fingerprints to the municipality to be sent to the FBI.
- A criminal history background investigation is required as part of the application for a license for insurance agents, title insurance agents, and title insurers. The investigation is conducted through fingerprint checks with the Department of Public Safety and the FBI. The same check may be used to suspend or revoke an insurer's license.

New Mexico Stat. 56.3.2 56.3.8 56.3.6
New Mexico Stat. 56.3.1
New Mexico Stat. 56.3.4
    1. Reports information
    2. Liability
    3. Definitions

SEARCHES AVAILABLE

- County Court Searches
- Sexual Offender
- Incarceration Records
- State Repository* (Notarized signed release required)

New York

New York Correct. Law §§ 750 to 754; N.Y. Exec. Law § 296(16) along with others
- It is unlawful discrimination for an employer to ask about any arrests or charges that did not result in conviction, unless they are currently pending.
- Convictions. Employers with 10 or more employees may not deny employment based on a conviction unless it relates directly to the job or would be an "unreasonable" risk to property or to public or individual safety. NY CORRECT §752
- Employers may not consider misdemeanor convictions older than five years unless the person has also been convicted of some other crime within the past five years.
- Upon request, an applicant must be given, within 30 days, a written statement of the reasons why employment was denied.

- Agency guidelines for pre-employment inquiries: New York State Division of Human Rights, "Rulings on Inquiries (Pre-employment)" found at http://www.nysdhr.com/employment.html
- No person may be required to be fingerprinted as a condition of employment or of continuing employment. The prohibition does not apply to: employees of the state or its municipal subdivision; to employees of legally incorporated hospitals, supported in whole or in part by public funds or private endowment; to employees of medical colleges affiliated with the above mentioned hospitals or to employee of private proprietary hospitals; to employees of public art galleries or museums housing valuable object of art, precious metals or stones (at the discretion of the trustees or board); to inspectors and investigators of the Department of Agriculture and Markets; to deputy or under sheriffs; to school employees; to employees of private detective licensees; to employees of the National Security Exchange; or to farm labor contractors.
- A caregiver may provide a prospective employer with a set of fingerprints upon request, or two sets of fingerprints if the prospective employer also is requesting a criminal background check from the FBI. A caregiver is a person employed for 15 hours or more per week caring for a child or children.

LAWS OF NEW YORK
General Business Law, Chapter 20 Of The Consolidated Laws, Article 25—Fair Credit Reporting Act

New York Gen. Bus. Law. 380.380.s Art 25.380s
New York Gen. Bus Law 380.b(b)
New York Gen. Bus. Law.380.c
1. Definitions
2. Permissible dissemination §380-b
3. Disclosure
4. Disputes
5. Requirements on Users
6. Prohibited information
7. Compliance

SEARCHES AVAILABLE
- County Court Searches
- Sexual Offender
- Incarceration Records
- State Repository* (Released with court order, subpoena, to entities authorized by statute, or to the person of record. Fingerprints are required.)

North Carolina

NORTH CAROLINA GENERAL STATUTES ANNOTATED
Chapter 58. Insurance, Article 39. Insurance Information And Privacy Protection Act

- Various provisions listed for insurance, public utilities, childcare and more.
- Criminal record checks are permitted for individuals who are employed by or who apply for employment with the following: licensed hospitals, licensed nursing homes, licensed domiciliary care facilities, licensed home care agencies or hospices, licensed child placement agencies, licensed residential child care facilities, licensed area mental health, developmental disability and substance abuse authorities, licensed child day care facilities and registered and non-registered child day care homes that are regulated by the state and any other organization or corporation, whether for profit or nonprofit, that provides direct care or services to children, the sick, the disabled or the elderly. The employee or applicant must consent to the record check.
- An offer of employment by a licensed nursing home or contract agency of a nursing home to an applicant to fill a position that does not require the applicant to have an occupational license is conditioned on the applicant's consent to a criminal history records check. An offer of employment by a licensed home care agency or contract agency of a nursing home to an applicant to fill a position that requires entering the patient's home is conditioned on the applicant's consent to a criminal history record check. In addition, the change in employment status of a current employee of a licensed home care agency or contract agency of a nursing home from a position that does not require entering the patient's home to a position that requires entering the patient's home must be conditioned on the current employee's consent to a criminal history record check. An applicant who refuses to consent to a criminal history record check may not be employed. In addition, a home care agency or contract agency of a nursing home may not change a current employee's employment status from a position that does not require entering the patient's home to a position that requires entering the patient's home if the employee refuses to consent to a criminal history record check. The request for a criminal record check must be submitted to the Department of Justice within five business days of making a conditional offer of employment. All criminal history information received by the home or agency is confidential and may not be disclosed, except to the applicant as provided below. If an applicant's criminal history record check reveals one or more convictions of a relevant crime, the nursing home or contract agency of the nursing home must consider all of the following factors in determining whether to hire the applicant: (1) the level and seriousness of the crime; (2) the date of the crime; (3) the age of the person at the time of the conviction; (4) the circumstances surrounding the commission of the crime, if known; (5) the connection between the criminal conduct of the person and the job duties of the position to be filled; (6) the prison, jail, probation, parole, rehabilita-

tion and employment records of the person since the date the crime was committed; and (7) the subsequent commission by the person of a relevant offense. The fact that the applicant was convicted of a relevant offense alone may not be a bar to employment; however, the listed factors must be considered. If after considering the relevant factors, the decision is to not hire the applicant, then the nursing home or the contract agency may disclose information contained in the criminal history record check that is relevant to the disqualification to the applicant, but may not provide him or her a copy of the criminal history record.

- Similar requirements apply to applicants for employment by a licensed adult care home or by a licensed contract agency of an adult care home.
- Criminal record checks are required of applicants and employees of the Department of Human Resources who provide direct care for a client, patient, student, resident or ward of the Department. National criminal record checks, using fingerprints, are required of all persons who have not resided in North Carolina during the past five years.
- All applicants for licensing as registered nurses or licensed practical nurses must consent to a criminal history record check.
- Prospective employees of private protection services must undergo criminal records checks

SEARCHES AVAILABLE

- County Court Searches
- Sexual Offender
- Incarceration Records
- State Repository

North Dakota

- Agency guidelines for pre-employment inquiries: North Dakota Department of Labor, Human Rights Division, "Employment Applications and Interviews" found at http://www.state.nd.us/labor/publications/brochures.html
- Background checks are required for applicants for licensing as teachers. Fingerprints are required for state and FBI testing.
- The Department of Human Services must obtain a criminal history before licensing or approving a facility providing foster care for children or adults.

SEARCHES AVAILABLE

- County Court Searches
- Sexual Offender
- Incarceration Records
- State Repository
- Workers' Compensation Records

Ohio

Ohio Rev. Code §§ 2151.358 (I); 2953.33 along with others
- Employers may not inquire into any juvenile records that have been sealed. May not ask about any other sealed conviction or unsealed bail forfeitures unless question has a direct and substantial relation to job.
- Applicants may not be asked about arrest records that are expunged; may respond to inquiry as though arrest did not occur.
- Nursing homes, resident care facilities, county and district homes, homes for the aging, adult care facilities, adult day care programs, hospice care programs and home health agencies are required to conduct a criminal record check for each person under final consideration for employment in a position in which there is direct contact with older adults. The criminal record check is done through the Bureau of Criminal Identification and Investigation.
- Employers hiring child care personnel must obtain criminal background information about the applicants.
- Employers holding contracts with the United States or any of its departments or agencies that contain nondiscrimination clauses may require an employee or applicant for employment to furnish documentary proof of citizenship and may use fingerprint identification for security purposes.

SEARCHES AVAILABLE
- County Court Searches
- Sexual Offender
- Incarceration Records
- State Repository* (fingerprints and witnessed signed release required)
- Workers' Compensation Records

Oklahoma

Oklahoma Stat. tit. 22, § 19(F) along with others
- Employers may not inquire into any criminal record that has been expunged.
- If record is expunged, an applicant may state that no criminal action ever occurred. May not be denied employment for refusing to disclose sealed criminal record information.
- Prior to employment, every owner or administrator of a child care facility must arrange for a criminal history investigation for any employment applicant and for any adult residing in a child care facility that is licensed or approved by a child-placing agency and located in a private residence, to be conducted by the State Bureau of Investigation. If the applicant or resident has resided in Oklahoma for less than one year, the criminal history investigation must be obtained from the previous state of residence.

- Any person required to register pursuant to the Sex Offenders Registration Act is prohibited from providing services to children, working for an employer who provides services to children, or residing in a child care facility. Violations of the law are considered a felony, punishable by incarceration or a fine.
- Criminal arrest checks must be done by employers before employing or contracting with a nurse aide, or other person to provide nursing care, health related services or supportive assistance to any individual.

Oklahoma Stat. tit. 24.148
Oklahoma Statutes title 24.section 148
   1. Disclosure
   2. Definitions

SEARCHES AVAILABLE

- County Court Searches
- Sexual Offender
- Incarceration Records
- State Repository
- Workers' Compensation Records

Oregon

Or. Rev. Stat. §§ 181.555 to 181.560; 659A.030 along with others
- Before requesting information, employer must notify employee or applicant; when submitting request, must tell State Police Department when and how person was notified. May not discriminate against an applicant or current employee on the basis of an expunged juvenile record unless there is a "bona fide occupational qualification."
- Arrest records. May request information about arrest records less than one year old that have not resulted in acquittal or have not been dismissed.
- Convictions. May request information about conviction records.
- Before State Police Department releases any criminal record information; it must notify the employee or applicant and provide a copy of all information that will be sent to employer. Notice must include protections under federal civil rights law and the procedure for challenging information in the record. Record may not be released until 14 days after notice is sent.
- Agency guidelines for pre-employment inquiries: Oregon Bureau of Labor and Industries, Civil Rights Division, Fact Sheets, "Pre-Employment Inquiries" found at http://www.boli.state.or.us/civil/tarpreemp.html
- Public schools must and private schools may request criminal background information on subject individuals seeking employment from the state police and the Federal Bureau of Investigation, through the Department of Education. The Department of Education will charge $42 for the cost of acquiring and furnishing

the information. The school district or private school may recover the cost or a portion of the cost from the subject individual. If the criminal records check indicates that the individual was convicted of a relevant crime or made a false statement as to the conviction of a crime, the school district must not and the private school may decide not to employ the individual. If a subject individual refuses to consent to a criminal records check, refuses to be fingerprinted or falsely swears to the non-conviction of a crime, the school district must terminate the individual's employment or contract. Subject individuals include: (1) an individual applying for initial licensing as a teacher, administrator or personnel specialist who has not submitted to a criminal records check within the previous year with the Teacher Standards and Practices Commission; (2) an individual who is applying for reinstatement of a license as a teacher, administrator or personnel specialist whose license has lapsed for at least three years; (3) an individual who is applying for initial licensing as a certified school nurse; (4) a school district or private school contractor, whether part-time or full-time, or an employee of a school district contractor, whether part-time or full-time, who has direct, unsupervised contact with students, as determined by the school district or private school; (5) an individual newly hired, whether part-time or full-time, by a school district or private school in a capacity not described in (1), (2) or (3) above who had direct, unsupervised contact with children, as determined by the school district or private school; (6) an individual employee, whether part-time or full-time, of a school district in a capacity not described in (1), (2) or (3) above who has direct, unsupervised contact with children, as determined by the school district; (7) an individual who is registering with the Teacher Standards and Practices Commission for student teaching, practicum or internship as a teacher, administrator or personnel specialist, if the individual has not submitted to a criminal records check within the previous year with the Teacher Standards and Practices Commission for student teaching, practicum or internship as a teacher, administrator or personnel specialist; or (8) an individual who is a community college faculty member providing instruction at a kindergarten through grade 12 school site during the regular school day. Subject individuals do not include individuals described in (4), (5), (6) or (7) above if the individual or the individual's employer was checked in one school district or private school and is currently seeking work in another school district or private school, unless the individual lived outside the state during the period between the two periods of time working in the school district or private school.

- Child-care agencies may hire only persons ("subject individuals") who have been enrolled in the Criminal History Registry, established and maintained by the Child Care Division of the Employment Department. If an individual has been convicted of a crime relevant to their working with children or made a false statement as to their conviction of a crime, the Division will determine whether the individual may be enrolled in the registry. Individuals may be enrolled only if they have no criminal or child protective services history or if they have dealt with the issues and provided evidence of suitability for the registry. Individuals who refuse to consent to a criminal record check or refuse to be fingerprinted will not be enrolled in the registry. Subject individuals, for purposes of the Criminal History Registry are individuals who apply to be: (1) the operator or an employee of a child care or treatment program; (2) the operator or an employee of an Oregon pre-kindergarten program or parent-as-teacher program; (3) the operator or an employee of a federal Head Start program, regulated by the United States Department of Health and Human Services; (4) an employee of the Child Care Division of the Employment Department; (5) an individual in a child care facility who may have unsupervised contact with children, as identified by the Division; (6) a contractor or an employee of a contractor who provides early childhood special education or early intervention services; (7) a child care provider who is required to be enrolled in the Criminal History Registry by any state agency; or (8) enrolled in the Criminal History Registry.

- For purposes of licensing, certifying, registering or otherwise regulating or administering programs for caregivers, a criminal record check, including fingerprint identification, must be conducted on all individuals that provide care, treatment, education, training, instruction, supervision, placement services, recreation or support to children, the elderly or persons with disabilities. Individuals that are determined to be unfit may not be employed, licensed, certified or registered. Individuals may, however, be hired on a probationary basis, pending the results of a criminal background check. Refusing to consent to a criminal background check will result in a denial or termination of employment.
- Applicants for certification as private security officers are subject to fingerprinting and a nation wide criminal records check.
- Pharmacy technicians must renew their registrations annually and provide, among other information, updated information regarding work history and criminal arrest and conviction history.

1. Disclosure
2. Definitions

SEARCHES AVAILABLE

- County Court Searches
- Sexual Offender
- Incarceration Records
- State Repository

Pennsylvania

18 Pennsylvania Cons. Stat. § 9125 along with others
- Employers may consider felony and misdemeanor convictions only if they directly relate to person's suitability for the job.
- Applicants must be informed in writing if the refusal to hire is based on criminal record information.
- Agency guidelines for pre-employment inquiries: Pennsylvania Human Relations Commission, Publications, "Pre-Employment Inquiries" found at http://sites.state.pa.us/PA_Exec/PHRC/publications/other_publications.html
- All prospective employees of public and private schools, intermediate units and area vocational-technical schools, including independent contractors and their employees, must submit with their employment application conviction data from the Pennsylvania State Police or a statement from them that no such data exists for that person.

SEARCHES AVAILABLE
- County Court Searches
- Sexual Offender
- Incarceration Records
- State Repository*(Special form required)
- Workers' Compensation Records

Rhode Island

- Arrest records. It is unlawful to include on an application form or to ask as part of an interview if the applicant has ever been arrested or charged with any crime.
- Convictions. May ask if applicant has been convicted of a crime.
- Applicants must be informed in writing of any disqualifying information found in the background check. Employers are required to keep on file evidence that criminal background checks have been obtained for all employees as well as the results of the checks.
- Applicants for employment in facilities licensed or registered with the department of health whose employment will involve routine contact with a patient or resident without the presence of other employees must undergo a statewide criminal background check prior to or within one week of employment.
- child care facility operators, employees and job applicants with supervisory or disciplinary authority over children and whose work involves regular contact with children without the presence of other employees, are subject to a nationwide criminal record check, including the taking of fingerprints. All youth serving agency operators, employees and job applicants, including recreation camp personnel, are also subject to criminal record checks prior to employment.

- Employers in public elementary and secondary school must incorporate criminal history background checks into their hiring practices. Background check is required for any employee who will have direct supervision or disciplinary power over children or routine contact with children without the presence of other employees. Background checks must be instituted within one week of a conditional job offer. Background checks are made through local police departments or the Bureau of Criminal Identification (BCI). Fingerprinting is not required.
- Employers must retain records showing that the background checks were instituted and the results of the background checks. If an employee underwent a background check in the previous 18 months, the employer may request a letter from the local police or BCI explaining the results, rather than instituting a new background check.
- Fingerprinting is required as part of a background and criminal record check for certification of personnel who provide services to very young children, including owners and operators of preschool programs and full-time or part-time employees, such as teachers, aides, secretaries, food handlers, bus drivers, volunteers and student teachers. Applicant's fingerprint cards must promptly be destroyed at the conclusion of the background or criminal background check.
- Individuals 18 years and older seeking employment in any facility or program licensed or funded by the Department of Mental Health, Retardation and Hospitals, will be required to undergo national criminal background checks to determine whether they have been convicted of a crime that bears upon their fitness to be responsible for the safety and well-being of the persons residing in or receiving services from the programs or facilities.

Rhode Island Gen. Laws. §6.13.1.20.6.13.1.21(a)
Rhode Island Gen. Laws §6.13.1.20(2) (1)
Rhode Island §6.13.1.27
Rhode Island General Laws. §6.13.1.21(a)
Rhode Island General Laws §6.13.1.21(b)

SEARCHES AVAILABLE

- County Court Searches
- Sexual Offender
- Incarceration Records
- State Repository

South Carolina

- Any person who has a criminal offense discharged, dismissed, or is found guilty can have all records of the arrest destroyed and no evidence of such record shall be retained by any municipal, county, or state enforcement agency. SC ST §17-1-40

- No person may be refused an authorization to practice, pursue, or engage in a regulated profession solely because of a prior criminal conviction unless it relates directly to the profession or occupation. SC ST §40-1-140
- In order to be employed by or to provide caregiver services at a licensed day care facility, an applicant must first undergo a state fingerprint review to determine any state criminal history and a fingerprint review by the Federal Bureau of Investigation to determine any other criminal history.
- Unless otherwise required by law, criminal history checks are not required for volunteers or for certified education personnel who have undergone criminal records checks as part of the certification process.
- Fingerprinting of candidates for training as law enforcement officers is required. In addition, fingerprinting is required from employees in the private security industry who are required to register with the South Carolina Law Enforcement Division. A fingerprint review by the State Law Enforcement Division and the FBI is required.

SEARCHES AVAILABLE

- County Court Searches
- Sexual Offender
- Incarceration Records
- State Repository
- Workers' Compensation Records

South Dakota

- Applicants for child welfare licenses, current and prospective employees of the Juvenile Division of the Department of Corrections or any adolescent treatment program operated by the Department of Human Services, and current and prospective employees of a school district must undergo criminal records investigations
- Agency guidelines for pre-employment inquiries: South Dakota Division of Human Rights, "Pre-employment Inquiry Guide" found at http://www.state.sd.us/dol/boards/hr/preemplo.htm

SEARCHES AVAILABLE

- County Court Searches
- Sexual Offender
- Incarceration Records
- State Repository* (fingerprints required)
- Workers' Compensation Records

Tennessee

- Home health services and child welfare agencies may require any person applying for employment, either as a paid employee or volunteer, to agree to the release of investigative records for the purpose of verifying the accuracy of criminal violation information contained on their work application. Applicants may also be required to supply fingerprint samples, or submit to a criminal history record check.
- Requires all employees who have direct contact with, or direct responsibility for individuals with developmental disabilities, supply a fingerprint sample for purposes of a criminal background check to determine if prior criminal convictions exist. The cost paid for by the employer.
- Adult day care center personnel are subject to criminal background checks.
- The Tennessee Bureau of Investigation is responsible for conducting criminal history checks for licensing security guards.

Tennessee Code. 47.18.1001.1011
1. Definitions
2. Disclosure
3. Adverse action

SEARCHES AVAILABLE
- County Court Searches
- Sexual Offender
- Incarceration Records
- State Repository
- Workers' Compensation Records

Texas

Texas Health & Safety Code § 765.001 and following; Tex. Gov't. Code § 411.118 along with others
- Special situations: A criminal background check is permitted upon a conditional offer of employment in a private "residential dwelling project," which includes a condominium, apartment building, hotel, motel or bed and breakfast, where the employee may be reasonably required to have access to residential units. Applicant must give written consent to release of criminal record information.
- Personnel at facilities caring for the elderly and disabled, employees of agencies that provide child care services, and public and private school personnel are required to undergo criminal background checks.

- Applicants for security sensitive positions at institutions of higher education may be required to submit criminal history information.
- Article 42.12. [781d] Community supervision - Deferred Adjudication; Community Supervision
  - Sec. 5. (a) Except as provided by Subsection (d) of this section, when in the judge's opinion the best interest of society and the defendant will be served, the judge may, after receiving a plea of guilty or plea of nolo contendere, hearing the evidence, and finding that it substantiates the defendant's guilt, defer further proceedings without entering an adjudication of guilt, and place the defendant on community supervision. A judge may place on community supervision under this section a defendant charged with an offense under Section 21.11, 22.011, or 22.021, Penal Code, regardless of the age of the victim, or a defendant charged with a felony described by Section 13B(b) of this article, only if the judge makes a finding in open court that placing the defendant on community supervision is in the best interest of the victim. The failure of the judge to find that deferred adjudication is in the best interest of the victim is not grounds for the defendant to set aside the plea, deferred adjudication, or any subsequent conviction or sentence. After placing the defendant on community supervision under this section, the judge shall inform the defendant orally or in writing of the possible consequences under Subsection (b) of this section of a violation of community supervision. If the information is provided orally, the judge must record and maintain the judge's statement to the defendant. The failure of a judge to inform a defendant of possible consequences under Subsection (b) of this section is not a ground for reversal unless the defendant shows that he was harmed by the failure of the judge to provide the information. In a felony case, the period of community supervision may not exceed 10 years. For a defendant charged with a felony under Section 21.11, 22.011, or 22.021, Penal Code, regardless of the age of the victim, and for a defendant charged with a felony described by Section 13B(b) of this article, the period of community supervision may not be less than five years. In a misdemeanor case, the period of community supervision may not exceed two years. A judge may increase the maximum period of community supervision in the manner provided by Section 22(c) or 22A of this article. The judge may impose a fine applicable to the offense and require any reasonable conditions of community supervision, including mental health treatment under Section 11(d) of this article that a judge could impose on a defendant placed on community supervision for a conviction that was probated and suspended, including confinement. The provisions of Section 15 of this article specifying whether a defendant convicted of a state jail felony is to be confined in a county jail or state jail felony facility and establishing the minimum and maximum terms of confinement as a condition of community supervision apply in the same manner to a defendant placed

on community supervision after pleading guilty or nolo contendere to a state jail felony. However, upon written motion of the defendant requesting final adjudication filed within 30 days after entering such plea and the deferment of adjudication, the judge shall proceed to final adjudication as in all other cases.

(b) On violation of a condition of community supervision imposed under Subsection (a) of this section, the defendant may be arrested and detained as provided in Section 21 of this article. The defendant is entitled to a hearing limited to the determination by the court of whether it proceeds with an adjudication of guilt on the original charge. No appeal may be taken from this determination. After an adjudication of guilt, all proceedings, including assessment of punishment, pronouncement of sentence, granting of community supervision, and defendant's appeal continue as if the adjudication of guilt had not been deferred. A court assessing punishment after an adjudication of guilt of a defendant charged with a state jail felony may suspend the imposition of the sentence and place the defendant on community supervision or may order the sentence to be executed, regardless of whether the defendant has previously been convicted of a felony.

(c) On expiration of a community supervision period imposed under Subsection (a) of this section, if the judge has not proceeded to adjudication of guilt, the judge shall dismiss the proceedings against the defendant and discharge him. The judge may dismiss the proceedings and discharge a defendant, other than a defendant charged with an offense requiring the defendant to register as a sex offender under Chapter 62, as added by Chapter 668, Acts of the 75th Legislature, Regular Session, 1997, prior to the expiration of the term of community supervision if in the judge's opinion the best interest of society and the defendant will be served. The judge may not dismiss the proceedings and discharge a defendant charged with an offense requiring the defendant to register under Chapter 62, as added by Chapter 668, Acts of the 75th Legislature, Regular Session, 1997. Except as provided by Section 12.42(g), Penal Code, a dismissal and discharge under this section may not be deemed a conviction for the purposes of disqualifications or disabilities imposed by law for conviction of an offense. For any defendant who receives a dismissal and discharge under this section:

(1) upon conviction of a subsequent offense, the fact that the defendant had previously received community supervision with a deferred adjudication of guilt shall be admissible before the court or jury to be considered on the issue of penalty;

(2) if the defendant is an applicant for a license or is a licensee under Chapter 42, Human Resources Code, the Texas Department of Human Services may consider the fact that the defendant previously

has received community supervision with a deferred adjudication of guilt under this section in issuing, renewing, denying, or revoking a license under that chapter; and

   (3) if the defendant is a person who has applied for registration to provide mental health or medical services for the rehabilitation of sex offenders, the Interagency Council on Sex Offender Treatment may consider the fact that the defendant has received community supervision under this section in issuing, renewing, denying, or revoking a license or registration issued by that council.

(d) In all other cases the judge may grant deferred adjudication unless:

   (1) the defendant is charged with an offense:

      (A) under Section 49.04, 49.05, 49.06, 49.07, or 49.08, Penal Code; or

      (B) for which punishment may be increased under Section 481.134(c), (d), (e), or (f), Health and Safety Code, if it is shown that the defendant has been previously convicted of an offense for which punishment was increased under any one of those subsections; or

   (2) the defendant:

      (A) is charged with an offense under Section 21.11, 22.011, or 22.021, Penal Code, regardless of the age of the victim, or a felony described by Section 13B(b) of this article; and

      (B) has previously been placed on community supervision for any offense under Paragraph (A) of this subdivision.

(e) If a judge places on community supervision under this section a defendant charged with an offense under Section 20.02, 20.03, or 20.04, Penal Code, or an attempt, conspiracy, or solicitation to commit one of those offenses, the judge shall make an affirmative finding of fact and file a statement of that affirmative finding with the papers in the case if the judge determines that the victim or intended victim was younger than 17 years of age at the time of the offense.

(f) A record in the custody of the court clerk regarding a case in which a person is granted deferred adjudication is not confidential.

(g) If a judge places on community supervision under this section a defendant charged with an offense under Section 21.11, 22.011, 22.021, or 43. 25, Penal Code, the judge shall make an affirmative finding of fact and file a statement of that affirmative finding with the papers in the case if the judge determines that:

   (1) at the time of the offense, the defendant was younger than 19 years of age and the victim or intended victim was at least 13 years of age; and

(2) the charge to which the plea is entered under this section is based solely on the ages of the defendant and the victim or intended victim at the time of the offense.

Liability For Negligent Hiring By In-Home Service Companies And Residential Delivery Companies

H.B. No. 705 was enacted on June 18, 2003 relating to liability of in-home service companies and residential delivery companies for negligent hiring. It amended SECTION 1. Title 6, Civil Practice and Remedies Code, by adding Chapter 145 to read as follows:

Sec. 145.001. DEFINITIONS. In this chapter: (1) "In-home service company" means a person who employs a person to enter another person's residence and for a fee repair: (A) an appliance; (B) the residence's heating, air-conditioning, and ventilation system; (C) the residence's plumbing system; or (D) the residence's electrical system. (2) "Residential delivery company" means a person who employs a person to, for a fee: (A) deliver an item to another person's residence; and (B) enter the residence to place, assemble, or install the item.

Sec. 145.002. CRIMINAL HISTORY BACKGROUND CHECK. An in-home service company or residential delivery company shall obtain from the Department of Public Safety or a private vendor approved by the department and offering services comparable to the services offered by the department all criminal history record information relating to an officer, employee, or prospective employee of the company whose job duties require or will require entry into another person's residence.

Texas Bus. Code. 47.18.1001-1011
Texas Bus. & Com. 20.01.20.10 20 & 20.05
Texas Bus. & Com. 20.08.20.09.
Texas Bus. & Com. 20.02(c)
1. Permissible purpose §20.02
2. Fees
3. Reporting of information
4. Disputes
5. Civil Liability
6. Definition

SEARCHES AVAILABLE

- County Court Searches
- Sexual Offender
- Incarceration Records
- State Repository* (fingerprints and signed release required)

Utah

Utah Admin. R. 606-2 along with others
- Employers are not permitted to ask about arrests and there are restrictions on the use of expunged criminal records.
- Convictions. Asking about felony convictions is permitted, but is not advisable unless the felony may be related to the job.
- The dissemination of information from a criminal history record or warrant of arrest information is limited to: private security agencies; employers whose employees are responsible for the care, custody or control of children; employers whose employees will have fiduciary trust over money; and employers whose employees provide health care to children, vulnerable adults or the elderly. Before requesting criminal record information on an employee or potential employee, the employer must obtain a signed waiver from the employee about whom the information is being requested.
- No one with a felony conviction may provide child care, child placement services, foster care or institutional care in Utah state facilities or programs. The prohibition also covers individuals licensed to provide day care services.
- Applicants for a real estate license must submit fingerprint cards and must consent to a criminal background check. The cost of the background check is borne by the applicant. Any new license issued is conditional, pending completion of the background check. If the background check discloses that the applicant has failed to accurately disclose a criminal history, the license will be revoked.
- At the time of initial application and renewal for licensure, all health care facilities must submit the name and other identifying information for each person associated with the facility in a direct patient care position to the department of health. The department of health must then determine whether any individual associated with the facility in a direct patient care position has been found guilty of child abuse or neglect, or abuse of persons with disabilities or the elderly. The determination is required, regardless of whether the person was the subject of a criminal background check within the preceding three-year period. Individuals who have not resided in the state for five years must submit fingerprints for an FBI national criminal history record check. The cost of the FBI background check is charged to the licensee.
- In addition, health care facilities must have criminal background checks performed for new hires. The health care facility must submit to the Department of Health, within 10 days of the initial hiring of an individual who provides direct care to patients, that person's name and other identifying information (may include fingerprints). The requirement applies even if the individual has been subject to a criminal background check within the preceding three-year period.

Utah Labor Division Anti-Discrimination Rules, Rule R6062. "Pre-Employment Inquiry Guide" found at http://www.rules.utah.gov/publicat/code/r606/r606-002.htm
1. Compliance with FCRA
2. Definitions - FCRA

SEARCHES AVAILABLE

- County Court Searches
- Sexual Offender
- Incarceration Records
- State Repository* (fingerprints required)

Vermont

Vermont Stat. tit. 20, § 2056c along with others

- Only employers who provide care for children, the elderly and the disabled or who run postsecondary schools with residential facilities may obtain criminal record information from the state Criminal Information Center. May obtain record only after a conditional offer of employment is made and applicant has given written authorization on a signed, notarized release form.
- The release form must advise the applicant of their right to appeal any of the findings in the record.
- Criminal record and substantiated reports of child abuse record checks may be requested by owners or operators of certain licensed facilities for current employees and, after conditional job offers have been made, for prospective employees. The commissioner of education may obtain the conviction records of any person applying for an initial license as a professional educator and a superintendent or headmaster of an independent school may conduct a record check on applicants for headmaster positions.
- Employers that are entitled to obtain information must inform current or prospective employees that they have the right to appeal the accuracy and completeness of the record.
- Employers providing services to vulnerable classes; children, the elderly, or persons with disabilities, or secondary schools with student residential facilities, may obtain from the crime information center a Vermont criminal record and an out-of-state criminal record for any applicant who has given written authorization on a release form provided by the center. Employers must file user agreements with the center. Employers must make an offer of employment conditioned on the record check before they can obtain the criminal record check.

Vermont Stat. tit. 9 2480a 2480g

SEARCHES AVAILABLE
- County Court Searches
- Sexual Offender* (Authorized only for employers working with children, the elderly, or disabled)
- Incarceration Records
- Workers' Compensation Records

Virginia

Virginia Code § 19.2392.4 along with others
- Employers may not require an applicant to disclose information about any criminal charge that has been expunged.
- Need not refer to any expunged charges if asked about criminal record.
- Criminal record checks are authorized for the following employers: school boards for the purpose of screening individuals who are offered or accept public school employment; licensed nursing homes for adults, licensed district homes for adults and licensed adult day-care centers for the investigation of applicants for compensation employment; the Department of Mental Health, Mental Retardation and Substance Abuse Services and facilities operated by the Department, personnel in private preschool or nursery school programs, school bus drivers, hospital pharmacy employees, and employees of residential facilities for juveniles, for the purpose of determining an individual's fitness for employment.
- The governing boards or administrators of accredited private or parochial schools must require applicants who accept employment for the first time to provide personal descriptive information that will be forwarded, along with the applicant's fingerprints, to the FBI for the purpose of obtaining criminal history information. The law applies to elementary and secondary schools and to full-time, part-time, permanent and temporary employees.
- As a condition of employment, school boards of certain counties and cities that follow the executive form of government must require any individual who accepts employment to submit to fingerprinting which shall be forwarded to the FBI for a criminal background check.
- Fingerprinting is also required of employees in the private security industry who are required to register with the Department of Criminal Justice Services.
- All persons employed by the State Lottery Department must be fingerprinted as a condition of employment.

Virginia Code. 59.1.335.1 335.12
1. Definitions
2. Disclosure - insurance
3. Permissible Purpose §59.1-335.2

SEARCHES AVAILABLE
- County Court Searches
- Sexual Offender (Two lists: Crimes against minors, Sex Offender Registry Name Request)
- Incarceration Records
- State Repository

Washington

Washington Rev. Code §§ 43.43.815; 9.94A.640(3), 9.96.060(3), 9.96A.020; Wash. Admin. Code 16212140
- Employers who ask about arrests must ask whether the charges are still pending, have been dismissed or led to conviction.
- Convictions. Employer who obtains a conviction record must notify employee within 30 days of receiving it, and must allow the employee to examine it. May make an employment decision based on a conviction only if it is less than 10 years old and the crime involves behavior that would adversely affect job performance.
- If a conviction record is cleared or vacated, may answer questions as though the conviction never occurred. A person convicted of a felony cannot be refused an occupational license unless the conviction is less than 10 years old and the felony relates specifically to the occupation or business.
- Special situations: Employers are entitled to obtain complete criminal record information for positions that require bonding or that have access to trade secrets, confidential or proprietary business information, money or items of value.
- Washington agencies or facilities that provide care and treatment to vulnerable adults may consider the criminal history of an applicant for employment in a licensed facility when the applicant has one or more conviction for simple assault, assault in the fourth degree, prostitution or theft in the third degree and three or more years have passed between the most recent conviction and the date of application for employment or second degree theft or forgery if five or more years have passed between the most recent conviction and date of application for employment.
- Employers in Washington may obtain criminal record information only for specified purposes: employee bonding; preemployment and postemployment evaluation of employees who may have or have had access to information, money or items of value; or investigations concerning penal offenses committed by employees.
- Any person seeking employment in a school district or educational service district, including volunteers, and any contractor responsible for hiring employees who will have unsupervised access to children, must submit to a records check through the Washington state patrol criminal identification system.

CODE OF WASHINGTON
Title 19. Business Regulations-Miscellaneous, Chapter 19.182. Fair Credit Reporting Act

Washington Rev. Code 19.182.005.19.182.902
Washington Rev. Code 19.182.020 (2) 19.182
Washington Rev. Code 19.182.020 (2) (c)
Washington revised code sec. 19.182.080(7).
Washington Rev. Code 19.182.050(1)
Washington Rev. Code 19.182.110(1)
  1. Definitions §19.182.010
  2. Procuring §19.182.020
  3. Prohibited Information §19.182.040
  4. Liability §19.182.050
  5. Compliance §19.182.060
  6. Disclosure §19.182.070
  7. Disputes §19.182.090
  8. Fees §19.182.100
  9. Adverse Action §19.182.110

SEARCHES AVAILABLE

- County Court Searches
- Sexual Offender
- Incarceration Records
- State Repository

West Virginia

- West Virginia law requires applicants for licenses from the Department of Education to submit to criminal records checks and to submit a set of fingerprints for a background check. Homecare services and residential care facilities personnel are also subject to criminal history checks.
- Agency guidelines for pre-employment inquiries: Bureau of Employment Programs, "Pre-Employment Inquiry Guide" found at http://www.state.wv.us/BEP/Bepeeo/empinqu.htm

SEARCHES AVAILABLE

- County Court Searches
- Sexual Offender
- Incarceration Records
- State Repository* (fingerprints required)
- Workers' Compensation Records

Wisconsin

Wisconsin Stat. §§ 111.31 to 111.35 along with others
- It is a violation of state civil rights law to discriminate against an employee on the basis of a prior arrest or conviction record.
- Arrest records. May not ask about arrests unless there are pending charges.
- Convictions. May not ask about convictions unless charges substantially relate to job.
- Special situations: Exceptions include required criminal history background checks for employees of care and service residential facilities, including hospitals, personal care worker agencies, supportive home care service agencies, and temporary employment agencies that provide caregivers to another entity, child welfare agencies, foster and group homes, and day care centers.
- Employers are entitled to obtain complete criminal record information for positions that require bonding and for burglar alarm installers.
- Discrimination because of an arrest record is permitted when employment depends on the bondability of the individual under a standard fidelity bond or when an equivalent bond is required by state or federal law, administrative regulation, or established business practice of the employer. Refusing to employ or license, or suspending or barring from employment or licensing any individual who is subject to a pending criminal charge or has been convicted of any offense is permitted if the circumstances of the charge substantially relate to the circumstances of the particular job or licensed activity.

SEARCHES AVAILABLE
- County Court Searches
- Sexual Offender
- Incarceration Records
- State Repository

Wyoming

- Newly hired school district employees who may have access to minors may be required to submit to criminal history checks, which involve fingerprinting. Fees for applications and issuance of certification may include the cost of the criminal history check.
- Child and disabled care agencies must screen prospective employees and volunteers who may have unsupervised access to minors or disabled adults.
- Deputy coroners and employees of a county coroner may be required to provide fingerprints and other information necessary for a state and national criminal history background check.

SEARCHES AVAILABLE

- County Court Searches
- Sexual Offender
- Incarceration Records
- State Repository* (fingerprints and notarized waiver required)
- Workers' Compensation Records

Criminal Background Screening
For the Health Care Industry

Most states require nurse background checks for some long-term care or other health care workers taking care of elderly or disabled people. The same requirements apply to nursing home direct care workers such as nurse's aides and other unlicensed workers in nursing homes. At least 30 states cover home health care workers. A number of states cover workers in residential care homes, adult foster care homes, boarding homes, assisted living facilities, adult day care centers, other health facilities, and various other settings.

Mandated State Healthcare Criminal Background Check

Alabama

Applicable Law: Alabama Act 2000-775
Effective Date: 11/01/2000
Processed by: Alabama Dept. of Public Safety/Alabama Bureau of Investigation
Fingerprints Required: YES
Fee: $49
Summary: Alabama Law requires that a "Mandatory Criminal History Check" be conducted by every employer, child care facility, adult care facility, the Dept. of Human Resources, and child placing agency on every employment applicant, employee or volunteer of an employer, child care facility, adult care facility or child placing agency. Those subject to criminal background checks must submit 2 sets of fingerprints and sign a written consent to obtain criminal history background information
Recommendation: **Court record or state repository records may be searched; however, if a job category falls within the state statute, fingerprinting will be required.**

Alaska

Applicable Law: AS 47.33.100 Background Check: Assisted Living Homes
 AS 18.20.302 Background Check: Nursing Facilities
Processed by: Alaska Dept. of Public Safety
Fingerprints Required: YES
Fee: $59
Summary: Requires state/national, fingerprint based criminal background check for assisted living home employees and for nursing home employees
Recommendation: **Court record or state repository records may be searched; however, if a job category falls within the state statute, fingerprinting will be required.**

Arizona

Applicable Law: Arizona Revised Statute 36-411. Residential care institutions; home health agencies; fingerprinting; definitions
Processed by: Arizona Dept. of Public Safety
Fingerprints Required: YES
Fee: $46
Summary: Subject to legislative appropriations, as a condition of licensure or continued licensure of a residential care institution, a nursing care institution or a home health agency and as a condition of employment in a residential care institution, a nursing care institution or a home health agency, employees and owners of residential care institutions, nursing care institutions or home health agencies or contracted persons who provide direct care, home health services or supportive services and who have not been subject to the fingerprinting requirements of a health professional's regulatory board pursuant to title 32 shall have valid fingerprint clearance cards that are issued pursuant to title 41, chapter 12, article 3.1 or shall apply for a fingerprint clearance card within twenty working days of employment or beginning volunteer work except as provided in subsections F, G and H of this section. A health professional who has complied with the fingerprinting requirements of the health professional's regulatory board as a condition of licensure or certification pursuant to title 32 is not required to submit an additional set of fingerprints to the department of public safety pursuant to this section.

Individuals are required to get fingerprint clearance if they are going to be caregivers providing direct care for a resident of a nursing facility. This process requires fingerprint submission and the signing of a user agreement with the employer and the Department of Public Safety.
Recommendation: **Court record or state repository records may be searched; however, if a job category falls within the state statute, fingerprinting will be required.**

Arkansas

Applicable Law: Arkansas Code 20.33.203 Mandatory criminal records checks for applicants, Elder Choices providers, and employees.
Effective Date: Effective October 1, 1997
Processed by: Arkansas Dept. of Human Services, Office of Long Term Care/ Arkansas State Police
Fingerprints Required: NO *(State Check)* YES *(State and Federal Check)*
Fee: $20 *(State Check)* $24 *(State and Federal Check)*
Summary: The Office of Long Term Care administers the Long-Term Care Criminal Record Check program. This program requires certain long-term care employees to undergo criminal record checks prior to employment in a long-term care facility. Conviction of

certain specified crimes will result in an applicant being permanently barred from working in a long-term care facility. Other, lesser crimes can result in suspension from employment in a long-term care facility for ten (10) years. The Office maintains a database, or registry, of individuals who are excluded from employment.

Recommendation: **In order to perform background screening on any long-term care employee, the end user of the report must register directly with the Dept. of Human Services themselves in order to obtain a registry authorization number. With the issued number, the end user must conduct the search. The Office of Long Term Care advises that this service may not be outsourced.**

California

Applicable Law: Health and Safety Code 1522
Processed by: California Department of Justice
Fingerprints Required: YES
Fee: DOJ: $42 FBI: $24
Summary: The California Health and Safety Code requires a background check of all applicants, licensees, adult residents, volunteers under certain conditions and employees of community care facilities who have contact with clients. If the California Department of Social Services finds that an individual has been convicted of a crime other than a minor traffic violation, the individual cannot work or be present in any community care facility unless they request a criminal record exemption form the Community Care Licensing Division, Caregiver Background Check Bureau. CBCB also examines arrest records to determine if there is a possible danger to clients.

Recommendation: **Court record or state repository records may be searched; however, if a job category falls within the state statute, fingerprinting will be required.**

Colorado

Applicable Law: 27-1-110 - Employment of personnel - screening of applicants
Processed by: Colorado Bureau of Investigation
Fingerprints Required: YES
Fee: $24 (state) $25 (FBI)
Summary: Law applies to individuals that will be child caregivers, EMT's, anyone employed by the Dept. of Human Services or any facility operated by the Dept. of Human Services, state and veterans nursing homes

Recommendation: **CRA's are compliant with the law, using CBI system if only a statewide check is required.**

Connecticut

Applicable Law: Health & Safety -Sec. 19a-491b. Notification of criminal conviction or disciplinary action. Civil penalty. False statements. Criminal history records checks

Processed by: Dept. of Public Safety/ FBI

Fingerprints Required: YES

Summary: The Commissioner of Public Health shall require each initial applicant described in subdivision (1) of subsection (a) of section 19a-491a: to submit to state and national criminal history records checks. The criminal history records checks required by this subsection shall be conducted in accordance with section 29-17a.

Recommendation: **Court record or state repository records may be searched; however, if a job category falls within the state statute, fingerprinting will be required.**

Delaware

Applicable Law: 16 Del. C. ss 1141, 1142, 1145/ 19 DEL. C. §708 and 11 DEL. C. §8563/ 11 DEL. C. §8564

Processed by: State Bureau of Identification/DHSS

Fingerprints Required: YES

Fee: $54

Summary: State Law requires criminal background checks and drug tests of all applicants for nursing home employment in Delaware. No employer who operates a home health agency, or a management company or other business entity that contracts to provide services on behalf of a home health agency, may hire an applicant without obtaining a report of the persons entire criminal history record from the State Bureau of Identification and a report from the DHSS regarding its review of a report of the persons entire federal criminal record history. Conditional hires are allowed if the employer received evidence that the applicant has requested his/her state and federal criminal history record, and has been fingerprinted by the State Bureau of Identification. Results must be obtained from a drug screening prior to employment. However, when exigent circumstances exist and an employer must fill a position in order to maintain the required level of service, the employer may hire the applicant on a conditional basis when the employer receives evidence that the applicant has actually had the appropriate drug screening.

Recommendation: **Court record or state repository records may be searched; however, if a job category falls within the state statute, fingerprinting will be required.**

Florida

Applicable Law: Florida Statute 435.03 & 435.04

Processed by: Florida Department of Law Enforcement

Fingerprints Required: Level 1 NO, Level 2 YES

Fee: $23 (Level 1) $ 47 (Level 2)

Process Summary: Level 1 consists of a query of the FDLE database for the criminal arrest history of an individual. Examples of applicants that fall under Level 1: Direct Care Staff at Adult Day Care Centers, Assisted Living Facilities, Home Health Agencies, Home Medical Equipment providers, Hospice, Nursing Homes (Level 2 required in some cases) Level 2 consists of a search of the FDLE and the FBI databases for any criminal arrest information both state and nationally. This search is generally required for Owner/ Administrator positions or Financial Officers at Healthcare facilities.
Recommendation: **CRA's are currently compliant with the law for Level 1 screening**

Georgia

Applicable Law: 31-7-351
Processed by: GCIC/DHR/ORS
Fee: $15
Summary: Prior to hiring an employment applicant, each nursing home shall request a criminal record check from GCIC to determine whether the applicant has a criminal record. A nursing home shall make a written determination for each applicant for whom a criminal record check is performed. A nursing home shall not employ a person with an unsatisfactory determination.

(b) Any request for a criminal record check under this Code section shall be on a form approved by GCIC and submitted in person, by mail, or by facsimile request to any county sheriff or municipal law enforcement agency having access to GCIC information. The fee shall be no greater than the actual cost of processing the request. The law enforcement agency receiving the request shall perform a criminal record check for a nursing home within a reasonable time but in any event within a period not to exceed three days of receiving the request.

(c) Each application form provided by the employer to the employment applicant shall conspicuously state the following: 'FOR THIS TYPE OF EMPLOYMENT, STATE LAW REQUIRES A CRIMINAL RECORD CHECK AS A CONDITION OF EMPLOYMENT.'
Recommendation: **CRA's are currently compliant with the law, because preliminary records check is done by inquiry of the GCIC database without fingerprints, based on name, social security # & date of birth.**

Hawaii

Applicable Law: Hawaii Statute 846 Criminal History Record Checks
Processed by: Hawaii criminal justice Data Center/FBI
Fingerprints Required: YES
Fee: $25
Summary: The following agencies : The Department of Health on operators of adult foster homes or developmental disabilities domiciliary homes and their employees; the Department of Health on prospective employees , persons seeking to serve as providers, or

subcontractors in positions that place them in direct contact with clients when providing non-witnessed direct mental health services; the Department of Human Services on operators and employees of child caring institutions, child placing organizations, and foster boarding homes; the Department of Human Services on applicants to operate child care facilities, prospective employees of the applicant and new employees of the provider after registration and licensure; may conduct criminal history record checks on the personnel identified. The criminal history record check shall require the submission of fingerprints to the FBI for a national criminal history record check and to the Hawaii Criminal Justice Data Center for a statewide check which shall include non-conviction data. The information contained shall be used exclusively for the stated purpose for which it was contained.
Recommendation: **Law does not apply to nursing homes, home health care, etc.**

Idaho

Applicable Law: ID APA 16.05.06—Rules Governing Mandatory Criminal History Checks
Processed by: Idaho State Police
Fingerprints Required: YES
Fee: $28 for Volunteers $45 for all other individuals
Summary: A self-declaration and a criminal history check shall be required of Department *(The Idaho Department of Health and Welfare)* employees, volunteers, student interns, and any other persons who have direct contact with children or vulnerable adults & other individuals, including providers and contractors and their employees, volunteers and student interns and any other persons, who provide Department funded direct care services to children or vulnerable adults.

The criminal history check is a fingerprint based check consisting of a self-declaration, fingerprints of the individual, information obtained from the FBI, the National Criminal History Background Check System, Bureau of Criminal Identification, the statewide Child Abuse Registry, Adult Protection Registry, Sexual Offender Registry, and Medicaid S/Urs exclusion list
Recommendation: **CRA's can NOT be compliant with the law if screening applicants that fall under "Individuals subject to Mandatory criminal history checks", because fingerprints are required.**

Illinois

Applicable Law: Illinois Healthcare Worker Background Check Act
Processed by: IL State Police Dept.
Fingerprints Required: NO (for initial search)
Fee: $15
Summary: To require a person seeking employment as a health care employee, which includes hospitals, nursing homes, home health agencies, hospices, nursing agencies, life

care and community living facilities, day training programs or any employee involved in direct patient care to undergo a criminal background check processed by the IL State Police Dept. and must comply with the requirements of the Illinois Uniform Conviction Act. The UCIA provides that criminal history records check may be conducted with or without a positive fingerprint id. However, a fingerprint search will be commenced by the facility whenever an applicant, employee or nurse aide's UCIA criminal history record check indicates a conviction for committing or attempting to commit any offense listed in the HWBCA.

Recommendation: **CRA's are currently compliant with the law, submitting names to the Illinois State Police.**

Indiana

Applicable Law: Section IC 16-25-6; IC 16-27-2; IC 16-28-13
Processed by: Indiana State Police
Fingerprints Required: NO
Fee: $20
Summary: Limited criminal history reports are required for Hospice Owners, Operators, Employees & Volunteers; Home Health Care Operators and Workers; Nurse Aides and Other Unlicensed Employees

Recommendation: **CRA's are compliant with the law, by registering with the state of Indiana (Access Indiana) to access Limited Criminal History reports.**

Iowa

Applicable Law: 135C.33 - Child or Dependant adult abuse information and criminal records
Processed by: Iowa Dept. of Public Safety
Fingerprints Required: NO for Statewide, YES for National
Fee: $15
Summary: Beginning July 1, 1997, prior to employment of a person in a facility, the facility shall request that the department of public safety perform criminal and dependent adult abuse record checks of the person in this state. In addition, the facility may request that the Department of Human Services perform a child abuse record check in this state. A facility shall include the following inquiry in an application for employment: "Do you have a record of founded child or dependent adult abuse or have you ever been convicted of a crime, in this state or any other state?" If the person has been convicted of a crime under a law of any state or has a record of founded child or dependent adult abuse, the Department of Human Services shall perform an evaluation to determine whether the crime or founded child or dependent adult abuse warrants prohibition of employment in the facility. The evaluation shall be performed in accordance with procedures adopted for this purpose by the Department of Human Services.

Beginning July 1, 1998, this section shall apply to prospective employees of all of the following, if the provider is regulated by the state or receives any state or federal funding:

a. An employee of a homemaker, home-health aide, home-care aide, adult day care, or other provider of in-home services if the employee provides direct services to consumers.

b. An employee of a hospice, if the employee provides direct services to consumers.

c. An employee who provides direct services to consumers under a federal home and community-based services waiver.

d. An employee of an elder group home certified under chapter 231B, if the employee provides direct services to consumers.

e. An employee of an assisted living facility certified or voluntarily accredited under chapter 231C, if the employee provides direct services to consumers.

Recommendation: **CRA's are compliant if a letter is submitted to the Iowa Department of Public Safety, Division of Criminal Investigation with the following information: organization name, address, phone number, fax number, contact person and a brief explanation of the organization's mandate. The DCI will assess whether your organization meets the criteria of a qualified entity. If qualified, further information and instructions will follow.**

Kansas

Applicable Law: 65-5117 & 39-970
Processed by: Kansas Bureau of Identification
Fingerprints Required: NO
Fee: $30 ($20 for approved Caregivers by KBI)
Summary: The operator of a home health agency shall request from the Department of Health and Environment information regarding only felony convictions, convictions under K.S.A. 21-3437 and 21-3517, and amendments thereto, adjudications of a juvenile offender which if committed by an adult would have been a felony conviction, and adjudications of a juvenile offender for an offense described in K.S.A. 21-3437 and 21-3517, and amendments thereto, and which relates to a person who works for the home health agency or is being considered for employment by the home health agency, for the purpose of determining whether such person is subject to the provisions of this section. For the purpose of complying with this section, the operator of a home health agency shall receive from any employment agency which provides employees to work for the home health agency written certification that such employees are not prohibited from working for the home health agency under this section.

The operator of a home health agency shall not be required under this section to conduct a background check on an applicant for employment with the home health agency if the applicant has been the subject of a background check under this act within one year prior to the application for employment with the home health agency. The operator of a home health agency where the applicant was the subject of such background check may release a copy of such background check to the operator of a home health agency where the applicant is currently applying.

Recommendation: **CRA's can NOT be compliant with the law, because law states that the "operator"(client) have the Kansas Dept. of Health and Environment (KDHE) access criminal history information through KBI records. Under these laws, certain juvenile convictions would constitute a prohibition of employment, which is one reason for the requirement as KDHE can access juvenile records.**
Currently CRA's have direct access to the KBI system.

Kentucky

Applicable Law: 216.789 Prohibition against employing certain felons at long-term care facilities, in nursing pools providing staff to nursing facilities or in assisted-living communities—Preemployment check with Justice Cabinet—Temporary employment.
Processed by: Kentucky State Police Records Branch
Fingerprints Required: NO
Fee: $10
Effective: July 14, 2000
Summary: The Kentucky State Police Records Branch, Name Search Section, conducts background checks for employment, licensing, and other similar purposes, as authorized by the Kentucky Revised Statutes. There is a $10.00 fee charged for each background check, and they must be submitted in person, or by mail. No electronic transmissions or faxes are accepted for this service.

Recommendation: **CRA's are compliant with the law by using Request for conviction records; however the applicant needs to fill out and sign the form, as well as a witness.**

Louisiana

Applicable Law: Revised Statute 40:1300:51 & 40:1300:52
Processed by: Bureau of Criminal Identification
Fingerprints Required: NO for initial; YES if record is found
Fee: $26 (without fingerprints, additional $24 for fingerprint search)
Summary: Louisiana is limited to those serving children or working in nursing homes or home health care. Name checks will only be performed for eligible entities. The applicant must complete an authorization form. Fingerprint checks will be performed if further clarification of identity is required.

Recommendation: **CRA's are compliant with the law by requesting criminal history checks through the LA Bureau of Criminal Identification.**

Maine

Applicable Law: 1812-G Maine Registry of Certified Nursing Assistants
Processed by: Dept. of Human Services
Summary: The Maine Registry of Certified Nursing Assistants is established in compliance with federal and state requirements. The Department of Human Services shall maintain the registry.
Recommendation: **CRA's are compliant with the law by running names through the Maine Registry of Certified Nursing Assistants.**

Maryland

Applicable Law: Maryland Code Title 19-1901, 1902; Health Care Facilities, Adult dependant care programs, criminal history record checks and background checks. Title 5 §619: Criminal background investigation of employees of facilities caring for children and employees of adult dependant care programs.
Processed by: Criminal Justice Information System (Central repository)
Fingerprints Required: NO
Fee: $18 (state) $42 (FBI)
Summary: Before an eligible employee may begin to work for an adult dependant care program (defined as: Adult Day Care Facility; Assisted living program facility; a group home; a home health agency; a congregate housing service; residential service agency; alternative living unit; a hospice facility) each adult dependant care program shall, for each eligible employee: Apply for state criminal history records check or request a private agency to conduct a background check. If an adult dependant care program requests a private agency to conduct a background check, the private agency shall conduct a background check in each state in which the adult dependant care program knows or has reason to know the eligible employee worked or resided during the past 7 yrs.
Recommendation: **CRA's are compliant with the law by running a statewide check.**

Massachusetts

Applicable Law: MGL/6-172C Dissemination of criminal offender record information to agencies employing or referring individuals to provide services to elderly or disabled persons & 172E Dissemination of criminal offender record information to long term care facilities
Processed by: Criminal History Systems Board (CORI)
Fingerprints Required: NO
Fee: $25
Summary: Long term care facilities and agencies employing or referring individuals to provide services to elderly or disabled persons shall obtain all available criminal offender information concerning any such individual from the criminal history systems board prior to employing such individuals.
Recommendation: **CRA's are compliant with the law by registering with the MA Criminal History Systems Board and upon approval using the CORI system.**

Michigan

Applicable Law: Public Health Code 333.20173
Processed by: Michigan State Police
Fingerprints Required: YES, only for applicants who have not resided in Michigan for 3 years or more.
Fee: $30 (state) $54 (for state to submit to Federal)
Summary: The new Act applies to every nursing home, county medical care facility, hospital long-term care unit and home for the aged in Michigan. The background check requirement applies to individuals that regularly provide direct services to residents who applied for and are offered employment, independent contract, or clinical privileges after May 10, 2002. However, the individual, like all other employees and contractors, must agree in writing to inform the facility immediately if they are subsequently arrested or convicted of one or more of the criminal offenses covered by the new law.
Recommendation: **CRA's are compliant with the law ONLY with applicants that have resided in Michigan for 3 years or more.**

Minnesota

Applicable Law: 144.057 Background studies on licensees and supplemental nursing services agency personnel.
Processed by: Department of Human Services
Summary: New applicants, employees, and volunteers must have background checks before they start work, and current licensees, employees, and volunteers must be checked according to schedule specified in statutes and rules, depending on the working arrangement of the individual. If a background study is initiated by an applicant or license holder and the applicant or license holder receives information about the possible criminal or maltreatment history of an individual who is the subject of the background study, the applicant or license holder must immediately provide the information to the commissioner.
Recommendation: **CRA's can NOT be compliant with the law because each "entity" must register with the Dept. of Health and comply with the SNSA act which states that the Dept. of Human services is solely responsible for the background studies of individuals.**

Mississippi

Applicable Law: Mississippi Code 41-11-13
Processed by: State Dept. Of Health, Criminal Information Center, FBI
Fingerprints Required: YES
Fee: $50
Summary: A criminal history record check is required to be performed on 1) every new employee of a licensed facility who provides direct patient care or services and who is employed after or on July 01, 2003; 2) every employee of the licensed facility employed prior to July 01, 2003 who has documented disciplinary action by his or her employer. In

order to comply with the statute it is required that fingerprints be provided and submitted to the State Department of Health. The state agency will then forward the fingerprints to the Criminal Information Center (CIC) and FBI Database.

Recommendation: **Court record or state repository records may be searched; however, if a job category falls within the state statute, fingerprinting will be required.**

Missouri

Applicable Law: 210.921.1. RSMo
Processed by: Department of Health and Senior Services
Fingerprints Required: NO
Summary: Any person hired on or after January 1, 2001 as a child care worker or elder care worker , or hired after January 1, 2002 as a personal care worker, as defined in 210.900, subsection 2, RSMo, is required to make application for registration in the Family Care Safety Registry within 15 days of beginning employment. Such person fails to submit completed registration form to the Dept. of Health without good cause is guilty of a class B misdemeanor. The aforementioned registry offers several resources for screening:

1. State criminal check conducted by the Missouri State Highway Patrol
2. Child abuse/neglect records, maintained by the Division of Family Services
3. The Employee Disqualification List, Maintained by the Division of Senior Services
4. The Employee Disqualification registry maintained by the Department of Mental Health
5. Child-care facility licensing records, maintained by the Department of Health and Senior Services
6. Foster parent, residential care facility, and child placing agency licensing records
7. Residential living facility and nursing home licensing records, maintained by the Division of Senior Services

Recommendation: **CRA's can NOT be compliant with the law, because each "entity" needs to register with the Dept. of Health and Senior Services/EDL unit and have a pin # assigned to them.**

Montana

Summary: HOUSE BILL NO. 546 "AN ACT REQUIRING NURSING HOME WORKERS AND NURSING HOME ADMINISTRATORS TO HAVE A CRIMINAL HISTORY BACKGROUND CHECK FOR PROSPECTIVE EMPLOYMENT IN A NURSING HOME" introduced to amend sections 37-9-301 and 44-5-302 MCA......However Montana Code Annotated 2003, does not show amendments.

Nebraska

Applicable Law: No noted law found regarding healthcare worker background checks

Nevada

Applicable Law: NRS 449.179 Initial and periodic investigations of criminal history of employee or independent contractor of certain agency or facility.
Processed by: Central Repository for Nevada Records
Fingerprints Required: YES
Fee: $21
Summary: Within 10 days of hiring an employee or entering into a contract with an independent contractor, the administrator of, or the person licensed to operate, an agency to provide nursing in the home, a facility for intermediate care, a facility for skilled nursing or a residential facility for groups shall obtain 2 sets of fingerprints and a written authorization to forward the fingerprints to the central repository for Nevada records of criminal history for submission to the FBI from the employee. An employee or independent contractor shall be investigated at least once every 5 years. If the investigation has been completed within the past 6 months and it did not indicate that the employee had been convicted of any crime set forth in 449.188, such person is exempt from these requirements.
Recommendation: **CRA's can NOT be compliant with the law, because fingerprints are required.**

New Hampshire

Applicable Law: 151:2-d Criminal Record Check Required; requiring criminal conviction record checks for employees working in long-term care facilities and in home health care and for applicants for a license from the board of nursing.
Processed by: New Hampshire Department of Safety, Division of State Police
Fingerprints Required: NO
Fee: $10
Effective Date: July 1, 2003.
Summary: Every applicant selected for employment with a home health care provider licensed under RSA 151:2, I(b), including those which provide only homemaker services, shall submit to the employer a notarized criminal conviction record release authorization form, as provided by the division of state police, which authorizes the release of his or her criminal conviction record to the facility pursuant to RSA 106-B:14; provided, that the scope of employment includes the provision of services in a client's home or otherwise involves direct contact with a client.
Recommendation: **CRA's can NOT be compliant with the law, because a notary's signature and seal are required.**

New Jersey

Applicable Law: C.100 (c.26:2H-83) Nurses aides, etc - criminal background checks
Processed by: Division of State Police in the Division of Law and Public Safety
Fingerprints Required: YES

Fee: $18

Summary: Requires criminal history record checks for all certified nurse aides, personal care assistants and homemaker-home health aides; requires plan for similar checks to be conducted on other providers of home care services. To initiate a background check, submit to the Commissioner the applicant's name, address and fingerprint cards taken by a State or municipal law enforcement agency.

Recommendation: **CRA's are compliant with the law by using SBI 212B Criminal Background Check request form for Non Criminal Justice employment.**

New Mexico

Applicable Law: 7.1.9.8 Caregiver Employment Requirements
Processed by: Department of Health/ DPS/ FBI
Fingerprints Required: YES
Fee: $5

Summary: All applicants for employment to whom an offer of employment is made, or employees and caregivers employed by or contracted to a care provider must consent to and submit consent form documents, personal identification documents, fingerprints and fees required for a nationwide criminal history screening. Applicants who have submitted all completed documents and paid all applicable fees may be deemed to have conditional employment pending receipt of a written notice given by the Department as to whether the applicant has a disqualifying conviction.

Recommendation: **CRA's can NOT be compliant with the law, because fingerprints are required.**

New York

Applicable Law: Executive Law S 837-n. Criminal history information of caregivers
Summary: Only applies to caregivers of children

North Carolina

Applicable Law: 114-19, G.S. 131D-40 &G.S. 131E-265,122C
Processed by: NC State Bureau of Identification
Fingerprints Required: YES
Fee: $15 (state $24 (federal)

Summary: Nursing Homes and Home Care Agencies, Adult Care Homes, Mental Health, Developmental Disabilities and Substance Abuse Services shall provide the Dept. Of Justice, along with the request, the fingerprints of the individual to be checked if a national criminal history record check is required and a form signed by the individual to be checked consenting to the check of the criminal record and to the use of fingerprints. If a national record check is required the fingerprints of the individual shall be forwarded to the State Bureau of Investigation who, in turn shall forward a set of fingerprints to the FBI for a national check. Within 5 business days of making a conditional job offer of employment, the above facilities shall submit a request to the Dept. of Justice to conduct a state or national record check required by this section, or shall submit a request to a private entity to conduct a State Criminal History Record Check required by this section. Conditional employment is allowed if the following requirements are met: The facility must obtain the applicant's consent or fingerprint's card and the facility shall submit the request for a criminal record check no later than 5 business days after the applicant begins conditional employment.

Recommendation: **CRA's can NOT be compliant with the law, because fingerprints are required**

North Dakota

Applicable Law: Found laws applying to Group Homes (children) or residential child care facility & teachers

Ohio

Applicable Law: § 3701.881 Criminal records check of prospective employees responsible for child or direct care to older adult; when employment prohibited.
Fingerprints Required: YES
Fee: $15 (processed by the Bureau of Criminal Identification and Investigation)
Summary: Except as provided in division (I) of this section, the chief administrator of a home health agency shall request the superintendent of the Bureau of Criminal Identification and Investigation to conduct a criminal records check with respect to each applicant. If the position may involve both responsibilities for the care, custody, or control of a child and provision of direct care to an older adult, the chief administrator shall request that the superintendent conduct a single criminal records check for the applicant. If an applicant for whom a criminal records check request is required under this division does not present proof of having been a resident of this state for the five-year period immediately prior to the date upon which the criminal records check is requested or does not provide evidence that within that five-year period the superintendent has requested information about the applicant from the Federal Bureau of Investigation in a criminal records check, the chief administrator shall request that the superintendent obtain information from the Federal Bureau of Investigation as a part of the criminal records check for the applicant. Even if an applicant for whom a criminal records check request is required under this division presents proof that the applicant has been a resident of this state for that five-year period, the chief administrator may request that the superintendent include information from the Federal Bureau of Investigation in the criminal records check.

Recommendation: **CRA's can NOT be compliant with the law, because fingerprints are required.**

Oklahoma

Applicable Law: 63-1-1950.1. Criminal arrest check on certain persons offered employment

Processed by: Oklahoma State Bureau of Investigation

Fingerprints Required: NO

Fee: $15

Summary: Before any employer makes an offer to employ or to contract with a nurses aide or other person to provide nursing care, health-related services or supportive assistance to any individual except as provided by paragraph 4 of this subsection, the employer shall provide for a criminal arrest check to be made on the nurses aide or other person pursuant to the provisions of this section. If the employer is a facility, home or institution which is part of a larger complex of buildings, the requirement of a criminal arrest check shall apply only to an offer of employment or contract made to a person who will work primarily in the immediate boundaries of the facility, home or institution.

Recommendation: **CRA's are currently compliant with the law requesting Criminal History checks through the Oklahoma State Bureau of Investigation.**

Oregon

Applicable Law: ORS 181.537/1, 10b, 10d

Processed by: Oregon Department of Human Services

Fingerprints Required: NO for State; YES if circumstances apply

Fee: $12

Summary: A subject individual must not be allowed to work, volunteer, be trained or reside in a facility or other environment identified in these rules without first completing and submitting to the Department (Oregon Department of Human Services or any subdivision thereof) a Criminal History Release Authorization form. A subject individual must not be allowed to work, volunteer, be trained or reside in a facility or other environment identified in these rules after having been found "unfit" pursuant to these rules. This includes environments in which the Department is directly or indirectly providing reimbursement or oversight for the provision of any services. A subject individual must complete a national criminal history check under any of the following circumstances: 1) Out of State Residency. If the subject individual has lived outside Oregon for 60 or more continuous/contiguous days during the previous three years. 2) Multi-state Offender. If the LEDS check, or any other information obtained by the Department indicates there may be criminal history outside of Oregon, or if the subject individual self-discloses criminal history outside of Oregon. 3) Identity or History Questioned. If the social security number is not provided to the Department, if the state check reveals a recent out-of-state driver's license, or if the Department has other reason to question the identity or history of the subject individual.

Pennsylvania

Applicable Law: Chapter 5 of the Older Adults Protective Services; (35 P.S. § 10225.502(a)(1); 18 Pa. C.S.A. § 9109

Processed by: Pennsylvania State Police/FBI/PA Department of Aging

Fingerprints Required: YES, if applicant is not a resident of PA or has not been a resident for the entire 2 years preceding the employment application

Fee: $24 (processed by PA Department of Aging)

Summary: The Older Adults Protective Services Act requires administrators and employees of nursing homes, personal care homes, domiciliary care homes, adult day care centers, and home health care providers to: Submit criminal background checks as a condition for employment.

The criminal background check requirement is that all facility applicants must submit with their employment application a criminal history report from the Pennsylvania State Police (35 P.S. § 10225.502(a)(1); see 18 Pa. C.S.A. § 9109). If the applicant is not a resident of Pennsylvania, or has not been a resident of Pennsylvania for the entire two years immediately preceding employment application, then in addition to the report from the PA State Police, a report of Federal criminal history record information must be obtained from the Federal Bureau of Investigation through the PA Department of Aging which has been designated by statute as the intermediary (35 P.S. § 10225.502(a)(2); see 28 U.S.C.A. § 534(a)(1)). A facility employee who has continuously been employed at the same facility before and since July 1, 1998 shall not be required to obtain the criminal background check as a condition of continued employment in that facility (35 P.S. § 10225.508(1)).

Recommendation: **CRA's can NOT be compliant with the law, because fingerprints are required.**

Rhode Island

Applicable Law: 23-17-34. Criminal records review — Nursing facilities — Home nursing care providers and home care providers.

Processed by: Bureau of Criminal Identification of the State Police

Fingerprints Required: Fingerprints NOT required.

Fee: Cost for Criminal Check $5

Summary: Any person seeking employment in a nursing facility, a home nursing care provider, or a home care provider which is or is required to be licensed, registered or certified with the Department of Health if that employment involves routine contact with a patient or resident without the presence of other employees, shall undergo a criminal background check to be initiated prior to or within one week of employment. All employees hired prior to the anactment of this section shall be exempted from the requirements of this section. The director of the department of health may by rule identify those positions requiring criminal background checks. The identified employee, through the employer, shall apply to the Bureau of Criminal Identification of the State Police or local police department for a statewide criminal records check. Fingerprinting shall not be required. Upon the discovery of any disqualifying information as defined in §23-17-37 and in accordance with the rule promulgated by the director of health, the Bureau of Criminal Identification of the State Police or the local police department will inform the applicant, in writing, of the nature of the disqualifying information; and, without disclosing the nature of the disqualifying information, will notify the employer, in writing, that disqualifying information has been discovered.

An employee against whom disqualifying information has been found may request that a copy of the criminal background report be sent to the employer who shall make a judgment regarding the continued employment of the employee. In those situations in which no disqualifying information has been found, the Bureau of Criminal Identification of the State Police or the employer shall maintain on file, subject to inspection by the department of health, evidence that criminal records checks have been initiated on all employees seeking employment after October 1, 1991, and the results of the checks. Failure to maintain that evidence would be grounds to revoke the license or registration of the employer.

Recommendation: **CRA's can NOT be compliant with the law, because fingerprints are required.**

South Carolina

Applicable Law: Article 23 Section 44-7-2910

Processed by: Criminal record checks required pursuant to this article must be conducted by the State Law Enforcement Division or by a private business, organization, or association which conducts background checks if that entity utilizes current criminal records obtained from the State Law Enforcement Division or the Federal Bureau of Investigation to determine any criminal record.

Fingerprints Required: NO, if it is verified that applicant has been a SC resident for the past 12 months; YES, if residency can not be verified.

Fee: $25 without fingerprints

Summary: (A) No direct care entity may employ or contract with a direct caregiver until after the direct caregiver has undergone a criminal record check as provided in this section. However, pending the results of the criminal record check, a person temporarily may be employed or may contract as a direct caregiver with a direct care entity. A direct care entity may consider the information revealed by a criminal record check as a factor in evaluating a direct caregiver's application to be employed by or contract with the entity.

Direct care entity means: a nursing home, a daycare facility for adults, a home health agency, community residential care facility.

Direct caregiver or caregiver means: a registered nurse, licensed practical nurse, or certified nurse assistant; Any other licensed professional employed by or contracting with a direct care entity who provides to patients or clients direct care or services and includes, but is not limited to, a physical, speech, occupational, or respiratory care; a person who is not licensed but provides physical assistance or care to a patient or client served by a direct care entity; person employed by or under contract with a direct care entity who works within any building housing patients or clients; a person employed by or under contract with by a direct care entity whose duties include the possibility of patient or client contact.

A direct care entity unable to verify South Carolina residency for a direct care applicant for the preceding twelve months shall conduct a federal criminal record check on the applicant in addition to the state criminal record check. However, if the direct care entity is located in a county of this State that borders either North Carolina or Georgia and the direct care applicant can verify residency in North Carolina or Georgia for the twelve months preceding the date of the employment application through the same means enumerated in (C)(1)(a) through (d), the direct care entity shall conduct only a state criminal record check in the applicant's resident state.

An applicant shall submit with the application one complete set of the applicant's fingerprints on forms specified or furnished by the State Law Enforcement Division. Fingerprint cards submitted to the State Law Enforcement Division pursuant to this section must be used to facilitate a national criminal record check, as required by this section. Pending the results of the criminal record check, a person temporarily may be employed or contract with a direct care entity. The criminal record check is not required to be repeated as long as the person remains employed by or continues to contract with a direct care entity; however, if a person is not employed by or is not under contract for one year or longer with a direct care entity, the criminal record check must be repeated before resuming employment or contracting with a direct care entity.

Recommendation: **CRA's can be compliant with law, if only a state search is required.**

South Dakota

Summary: Background check laws apply to employees of child welfare agencies and teachers

Tennessee

Effective Date: 01/01/2004
Applicable Law: Tenn. Code 68-11-256
Processed by: Tennessee Bureau of Investigation/FBI
Fingerprints Required: YES
Fee: $24 (state) $48 (state and federal)

Summary: All nursing homes shall initiate a criminal background check on any person who is employed in a position which involves providing direct care to a resident or patient prior to or within 7 days of employment. "Nursing home" means any institution, place, building or agency represented and held out to the general public for the express or implied purpose of providing care for one or more persons who are not related and are not acutely ill, but who do require skilled nursing care and related medical services.

Any person who applies for employment in such position shall consent to providing past work and personal references and/or, agree to the release of any and all information and investigative records necessary for the purpose of verifying whether the person has been convicted of a felony to either the nursing home or its agents, or to any agency that contracts with the state and/or supply a fingerprint sample and submit a criminal history records check to be conducted by the TN Bureau of Investigation, other law enforcement agency, or any legally authorized entity; and/or release any information required for a background check by a professional background screening organization.

Recommendation: **CRA's can NOT be compliant with the law, because fingerprints are required.**

Texas

Applicable Law: Health & Safety - CHAPTER 250. NURSE AIDE REGISTRY AND CRIMINAL HISTORY CHECKS OF EMPLOYEES AND APPLICANTS FOR EMPLOYMENT IN CERTAIN FACILITIES SERVING THE ELDERLY OR PERSONS WITH DISABILITIES; 250.004. Criminal History Record of Employees

Processed by: Department of Public Safety

Fingerprints Required: NO

Fee: $5

Effective: Sept. 1, 1999

Summary: Identifying information of an employee in a covered facility shall be submitted electronically, on disk, or on a typewritten form to the Department of Public Safety to obtain the person's criminal conviction record when the person applies for employment and at other times as the facility may determine appropriate. In this subsection, "identifying information" includes: the complete name, race, and sex of the employee; any known identifying number of the employee, including social security number, driver's license number, or state identification number; and the employee's date of birth. If the Department of Public Safety reports that a person has a criminal conviction of any kind, the conviction shall be reviewed by the facility to determine if the conviction may bar the person from employment in a facility under Section 250.006 or if the conviction may be a contraindication to employment.

Recommendation: **CRA's can be compliant with law, by requesting in writing a statewide search from the Department of Public Safety.**

Utah

Applicable Law: Utah Code Section 26-21-9.5
Processed by: Bureau of Criminal Identification
Fingerprints Required: Preliminary NO; YES if record is found or if individual has not had residency in Utah for the last five years
Fee: $10 (without fingerprints) $18 (with fingerprints)
Summary: Law requires that a BCI be conducted on covered individuals requesting to be licensed, to renew a license or to be employed or volunteer in a covered health facility. A request shall be submitted within 10 days of initially hiring the individual.
Recommendation: **CRA's can be compliant with initial state search and/or individual has had residency in UT for the last 5 yrs.**

Vermont

Applicable Law: Sec. 7. 20 V.S.A. § 2056c
Processed by: Vermont Crime Information Center
Fingerprints Required: NO
Fee: $10 if materials are not provided to the VCIC
Summary: Employer is a qualified entity that provides care or services to vulnerable classes as provided in 42 U.S.C. §§ 5119a and 5119c; "Vulnerable classes" means children, the elderly, and persons with disabilities as defined in 42 U.S.C. § 5119c.

An employer may obtain from the center a Vermont criminal record and an out-of-state criminal record for any applicant who has given written authorization on a release form provided by the center, provided that the employer has filed a user's agreement with the center.

Nothing in this section shall create a statutory duty for an employer to perform a criminal record check on every job applicant hired by the employer. An employer's failure to obtain a criminal record on an employee who subsequently commits a criminal offense shall not be the sole factor in determining civil or criminal liability unless otherwise authorized by law.
Recommendation: **Should you wish to obtain criminal history information from VCIC, we need the following materials:**

- A copy of the statute, executive order, municipal charter or ordinance, which denies licensing, employment or civil rights to a person convicted of a crime. If you are an agency that does applicant screening for various companies, VCIC requires a statute from the state in which the applicant has applied for employment.
- If the requirement to conduct a criminal record check is not specified in a statute, VCIC will accept documentation as to the employer's authority to obtain criminal history information.
- A user agreement and record release form must be filled out completely on company letterhead.
- A stamped self-addressed envelope is required.

VCIC has no requirement to submit fingerprints with criminal history requests.

Virginia

Applicable Law: Section 19.2-389 of the Code of Virginia
Processed by: Department of State Police Criminal Justice Information Services
Fingerprints Required: NO
Fee: $15 (processed by Department of State Police Criminal Justice Information Services)
Summary: Criminal history record information shall be disseminated, whether directly or through an intermediary, only to Licensed nursing homes, hospitals and home care organizations for the conduct of investigations of applicants for compensated employment in licensed nursing homes pursuant to § 32.1-126.01, hospital pharmacies pursuant to § 32.1-126.02, and home care organizations pursuant to § 32.1-162.9:1, subject to the limitations set out in subsection E; Licensed homes for adults, licensed district homes for adults, and licensed adult day-care centers for the conduct of investigations of applicants for compensated employment in licensed homes for adults pursuant to § 63.2-1720, in licensed district homes for adults pursuant to § 63.1-189.1, and in licensed adult day-care centers pursuant to § 63.2-1720, subject to the limitations set out in subsection F;

A nursing home shall, within 30 days of employment, obtain for any compensated employees an original criminal record clearance with respect to convictions for offenses specified in this section or an original criminal history record from the Central Criminal Records Exchange. The provisions of this section shall be enforced by the Commissioner. If an applicant is denied employment because of convictions appearing on his criminal history record, the nursing home shall provide a copy of the information obtained from the Central Criminal Records Exchange to the applicant.

A licensed hospital shall obtain, within sixty days of employment of any compensated employee of the hospital whose duties will provide access to controlled substances as defined in § 54.1-3401 within the hospital pharmacy, who is not licensed by the Board of Pharmacy, an original criminal history record information from the Central Criminal Records Exchange. The cost of obtaining the criminal history record information shall be borne by the hospital.

Such home care organization or hospice shall, within 30 days of employment, obtain for any compensated employees an original criminal record clearance with respect to convictions for offenses specified in this section or an original criminal history record from the Central Criminal Records Exchange. The provisions of this section shall be enforced by the Commissioner. If an applicant is denied employment because of convictions appearing on his criminal history record, the home care organization or hospice shall provide a copy of the information obtained from the Central Criminal Records Exchange to the applicant.

However, a home care organization or hospice may hire an applicant convicted of one misdemeanor specified in this section not involving abuse or neglect or moral turpitude, provided five years have elapsed since the conviction.

An assisted living facility, adult day care center or child welfare agency licensed or registered in accordance with the provisions of this chapter, or family day homes approved by family day systems, shall not hire for compensated employment persons who have an offense as defined in § 63.2-1719. Such employees shall undergo background checks pursuant to subsection C. In the case of child welfare agencies, the provisions of this section shall apply to employees who are involved in the day-to-day operations of such agency or who are alone with, in control of, or supervising one or more children.

Background checks pursuant to this section require:

1. A sworn statement or affirmation disclosing whether the person has a criminal conviction or is the subject of any pending criminal charges within or outside the Commonwealth and, in the case of child welfare agencies, whether or not the person has been the subject of a founded complaint of child abuse or neglect within or outside the Commonwealth;
2. A criminal history record check through the Central Criminal Records Exchange pursuant to § 19.2-389; and
3. In the case of child welfare agencies, a search of the central registry maintained pursuant to § 63.2-1515 for any founded complaint of child abuse and neglect.

Recommendation: **CRA's can be compliant with law, by submitting SP-230 Form for statewide check.**

Washington

Applicable Law: RCW 43.43.832
Processed by: Washington State Patrol/Child and Adult Abuse Information Act
Fingerprints Required: NO
Fee: $10
Summary: The legislature finds that businesses and organizations providing services to children , developmentally disabled persons and vulnerable adults need adequate information to determine which employees or licensees to hire or engage. Therefore the WSP Identification and Criminal History Section may disclose upon request, convictions of crimes against children or other persons, crimes relating to financial exploitation of a vulnerable adult and certain civil adjudications. Organizations who educate, train, treat, supervise house or provide recreation to children under sixteen years of age, developmentally disabled persons or vulnerable adults may do background checks on perspective employees, volunteers or adoptive parents. The background check is for initial employment or engagement decisions only. The requesting agency must notify the applicant of the WSP response.

Recommendation: **CRA's are currently compliant with the law using Washington WATCH On-Line search.**

West Virginia

Applicable Law: Code of State Rules 64-13-11.3 Criminal Background Checks
Processed by: Not specified
Fingerprints Required: NO
Summary: 11.3. Criminal Background Checks.

11.3.a. A nursing home shall conduct a criminal conviction investigation on all applicants for employment.

11.3.b. If an applicant has been convicted of a misdemeanor or a felony offense constituting child abuse or neglect or abuse or neglect of an incapacitated adult, he or she may not be employed by a nursing home.

11.3.c. An applicant may also not be employed by the nursing home if he or she is under indictment for, or convicted of, in any court of a crime punishable by imprisonment for more than one year or is a fugitive from justice.

Recommendation: Law vague, no recommendation can be concluded. Check with legal counsel.

Wisconsin

Applicable Law: Wis.s.50.065 Criminal history and patient abuse record search.
Processed by: Wisconsin Criminal Information Bureau
Fingerprints Required: NO
Fee: $15.50
CRA's Capability: YES - via internet using pre-established account
Summary: Caregiver entities required to do background checks under Wis. s. 50.065, and child care entities under s.48.685 may request both an inquiry into criminal files at CIB, and into other files at the Wisconsin Department of Health and Family Services and the Wisconsin Department of Regulation and Licensing.
Recommendation: CRA's are currently compliant with the law using Wisconsin On-Line Caregiver search.

Wyoming

Applicable Law: Act found; Died in Committee on 02/28/2002; No other laws found.

STATES WITH DRUG TESTING LAWS

The following is a summary of various state drug testing laws. Please note that these laws may change at anytime and one must consult legal counsel prior to making any changes in your procedures.

Alabama:

Restrictions: None
Specific Requirements: No mandatory drug testing laws; however, employers may wish to follow the procedures set forth in the Voluntary Workers' Compensation Premium Reduction Act (ALA. Code §25-5-51(2000)).

Pre Employment: Permitted
Random: Permitted
For Cause: Permitted
Post Accident: Permitted
MRO: None Required

Alaska:

Voluntary laws affecting drug and alcohol testing exist in Alaska. No cause of action may be brought against any employer that has established an alcohol or drug testing program in accordance with the law for adverse employment actions taken in good faith based on a positive drug or alcohol test.

Note: These rules are voluntary in order to receive a "shield" to certain types of litigation.

Pre Employment: Permitted
Random: Permitted
For Cause: Permitted. Employees making reasonable suspicion determinations must be trained to recognize drug use and alcohol misuse.
Post Accident: Permitted, if test is administered immediately following the accident.
MRO: All positives must be reviewed by an MRO.

Arizona:

Voluntary laws affecting drug and alcohol testing exist in Arizona. No cause of action may be brought against any employer that has established an alcohol or drug testing program in accordance with the law for adverse employment actions taken in good faith based on a positive drug or alcohol test.

Note: These rules are voluntary in order to receive a "shield" to certain types of litigation.

Pre Employment: Permitted
Random: Permitted
For Cause: Broadly permitted when there is reasonable suspicion and adversely affect job performance.
Post Accident: Permitted
MRO: None required

Arkansas:

Restrictions: None
Specific Requirements: No mandatory drug testing laws; however, employers may wish to follow the procedures set forth in the Voluntary Workers' Compensation Premium Reduction Act (ARK. Code Ann. §11-9-102(4)(B)(iv)(2002)).

Pre Employment: Permitted
Random: Permitted
For Cause: Permitted
Post Accident: Permitted
MRO: None Required

California:

Pre Employment: Permitted
Random: Safety sensitive and DOT only
For Cause: Permitted
Post Accident: Permitted
MRO: None required

San Francisco, California:

Pre Employment: Permitted
Random: Safety sensitive and DOT only
For Cause: Permitted
Post Accident: Prohibited
MRO: None required

Colorado:

Pre Employment: Permitted
Random: Safety sensitive (not specifically addressed for Boulder, Colorado) and DOT only
For Cause: Permitted
Post Accident: Permitted (not specifically addressed for Boulder, Colorado)

MRO: None required

Connecticut:

Pre Employment: Permitted
Random: Safety sensitive and DOT only
For Cause: Permitted
Post Accident: Prohibited
MRO: None required

Delaware:

Restrictions: None
Specific Requirements: None

District of Columbia:

Restrictions: None
Specific Requirements: None

Florida:

Restrictions: None
Specific Requirements: No mandatory drug testing laws; however, employers may wish to follow the procedures set forth in the Voluntary Workers' Compensation Premium Reduction Act (FLA. Stat. Ann. §440.101 (West 2002)).

Pre Employment: Permitted
Random: Permitted
For Cause: Permitted
Post Accident: Permitted
MRO: None Required

Georgia:

Restrictions: None
Specific Requirements: No mandatory drug testing laws; however, employers may wish to follow the procedures set forth in the Voluntary Workers' Compensation Premium Reduction Act (Ga. Code. Ann. §34-9-17 (1998)).

Pre Employment: Permitted
Random: Permitted
For Cause: Permitted

Post Accident: Permitted
MRO: None Required

Hawaii:

Pre Employment: Permitted
Random: Permitted
For Cause: Permitted
Post Accident: Permitted
MRO: All positive must be verified by an MRO and initial tests must be confirmed by GC/MS, or another comparable reliable method

Idaho:

Voluntary laws affecting drug and alcohol testing exist in Idaho. No cause of action may be brought against any employer that has established an alcohol or drug testing program in accordance with the law for adverse employment actions taken in good faith based on a positive drug or alcohol test.

Note: These rules are voluntary in order to receive a "shield" to certain types of litigation.

Pre Employment: Permitted
Random: Permitted
For Cause: Permitted
Post Accident: Permitted
MRO: None required

Illinois:

Pre Employment: Permitted
Random: Permitted
For Cause: Permitted
Post Accident: Permitted
MRO: None required

Indiana:

Pre Employment: Permitted
Random: Permitted
For Cause: Permitted
Post Accident: Permitted
MRO: None required

Iowa:

Pre Employment: Permitted
Random: Permitted
For Cause: Permitted
Post Accident: Permitted
MRO: Required review of any positive test result before it is reported to the employer.

Kansas:

Pre Employment: Permitted
Random: Permitted
For Cause: Permitted
Post Accident: Permitted
MRO: None required

Kentucky:

Pre Employment: Permitted
Random: Permitted
For Cause: Permitted
Post Accident: Permitted
MRO: None required

Louisiana:

Pre Employment: Permitted
Random: Permitted
For Cause: Permitted
Post Accident: Permitted
MRO: Required review of any positive test result before it is reported to the employer.

Maine:

Pre Employment: Permitted
Random: Permitted
For Cause: Permitted
Post Accident: Permitted
MRO: None required

Maryland:

Pre Employment: Permitted
Random: Permitted
For Cause: Permitted
Post Accident: Permitted
MRO: Required review of any positive test result before it is reported to the employer.

Massachusetts:

Pre Employment: Permitted
Random: Permitted
For Cause: Permitted
Post Accident: Permitted
MRO: None required

Michigan:

Pre Employment: Permitted
Random: Permitted
For Cause: Permitted
Post Accident: Permitted
MRO: None required

Minnesota:

Restriction: Employees who test positive ordinarily may not be discharged for a first positive test result.
Pre Employment: Permitted, if conditional job offer made prior to test, provided all applicants for same position are tested. If job offer is withdrawn, applicant must be informed of employer's reasons.
Random: Permitted, safety sensitive only. Safety sensitive is position in which impairment by drug use would threaten the health or safety of any person. An employee may not be waived once selected from random pool.
For Cause: Permitted, when there is reasonable suspicion that employee while at work: (1) is under influence of alcohol or controlled substance; (2) violated work rule prohibiting alcohol or controlled substance use while operating machinery; (3) sustain or caused injury to another person; (4) caused a work related accident or was involved in such.
Post Accident: Permitted, same as For Cause.
MRO: None required

Mississippi:

Specific Requirements: No mandatory drug testing laws; however, employers may wish to follow the procedures set forth in the Voluntary Employee Drug and Alcohol Testing Act and the Mississippi Drug-Free Workplace Workers' Compensation Premium Reduction Act (Miss. Code Ann. §71-3-7(2000)).

Pre Employment: Permitted
Random: Permitted
For Cause: Permitted
Post Accident: Permitted
MRO: None required

Missouri:

Pre Employment: Permitted
Random: Permitted
For Cause: Permitted
Post Accident: Permitted
MRO: None required

Montana:

Pre Employment: Permitted
Random: Permitted
For Cause: Permitted
Post Accident: Permitted
MRO: Required review of any positive test result before it is reported to the employer.

Nebraska:

Pre Employment: Permitted
Random: Permitted
For Cause: Permitted
Post Accident: Permitted
MRO: None required

Nevada:

Pre Employment: Permitted
Random: Permitted
For Cause: Permitted
Post Accident: Permitted
MRO: None required

New Jersey:

Pre Employment: Permitted
Random: Permitted
For Cause: Permitted
Post Accident: Permitted
MRO: None required

New Mexico:

Pre Employment: Permitted
Random: Permitted
For Cause: Permitted
Post Accident: Permitted
MRO: None required

New York:

Pre Employment: Permitted
Random: Permitted
For Cause: Permitted
Post Accident: Permitted
MRO: MRO on all results

North Carolina:

Pre Employment: Permitted
Random: Permitted
For Cause: Permitted
Post Accident: Permitted
MRO: None required

North Dakota:

Pre Employment: Permitted
Random: Permitted
For Cause: Permitted
Post Accident: Permitted
MRO: None required

Ohio:

Restrictions: None
Specific Requirements: No mandatory drug testing laws; however, employers may wish to conduct their programs in accordance with the administrative regulations adopted by the Ohio Workers' Compensation Commission.

Pre Employment: Permitted
Random: Permitted
For Cause: Permitted
Post Accident: Permitted
MRO: None required

Oklahoma:

Pre Employment: Permitted
Random: Permitted
For Cause: Permitted
Post Accident: Prohibited unless an employer has reasonable suspicion that property damage in excess of $500 or a work-related injury was the direct result of an employee's use of alcohol or drugs.
MRO: Must utilize a MRO to receive and evaluate test results in light of each individual's medical history or other medical information.

Oregon:

Pre Employment: Permitted
Random: Permitted
For Cause: Permitted
Post Accident: Permitted
MRO: None required

Pennsylvania:

Pre Employment: Permitted
Random: Permitted
For Cause: Permitted
Post Accident: Permitted
MRO: None required

Rhode Island:

Pre Employment: Permitted
Random: Prohibited
For Cause: Permitted when an employer has reasonable grounds to believe that drugs are imparing job performance. Must be able to point to specific aspects.
Post Accident: Prohibited, unless for-cause requirements are met.
MRO: None required

South Carolina:

Pre Employment: Permitted
Random: Permitted
For Cause: Permitted
Post Accident: Permitted
MRO: None required

South Dakota:

Pre Employment: Permitted
Random: Permitted
For Cause: Permitted
Post Accident: Permitted
MRO: None required

Tennessee:

Voluntary laws affecting drug and alcohol testing exist in Tennessee. The voluntary law provides a 5% discount on Workers Compensations premiums to employers who implement a drug-free work place program in compliance with the Workers Compensation Premium Reduction Act.

Note: These rules are voluntary in order to receive a 5% discount on WC premiums.

Pre Employment: Required following a conditional job offer.

Random: Permitted, but not required.
For Cause: Permitted, defined broadly. Reasons for the suspicion which led to test must be documented.
Post Accident: Permitted, if the accident resulted in injury.
MRO: All positives must be reviewed by an MRO.

Texas:

Pre Employment: Permitted
Random: Permitted
For Cause: Permitted
Post Accident: Permitted
MRO: None required

Utah:

Voluntary laws affecting drug and alcohol testing exist in Utah. No cause of action may be brought against any employer that has established an alcohol or drug testing program in accordance with the law for adverse employment actions taken in good faith based on a positive drug or alcohol test.

Note: These rules are voluntary in order to receive a "shield" to certain types of litigation.

Pre Employment: Permitted
Random: Permitted
For Cause: Permitted
Post Accident: Permitted
MRO: None required

Vermont:

Pre Employment: Permitted.
Random: Prohibited, except when required by federal law or regulation.
For Cause: Permitted.
Post Accident: Prohibited as general policy; but, permitted under very limited circumstances.
MRO: Required of all test results and must personally contact any individual who has a positive test result.

Virginia:

Pre Employment: Permitted
Random: Permitted
For Cause: Permitted
Post Accident: Permitted
MRO: None required

Washington:

Pre Employment: Permitted
Random: Permitted
For Cause: Permitted
Post Accident: Permitted
MRO: None required

*MRO Defined: Medical Review Officer - A designated person or company who reviews the laboratory results prior to providing final results to the employer. The MRO may decide to investigate findings further by contacting the subject of the drug test and reviewing prescriptions being used.

West Virginia:

Pre Employment: Permitted
Random: Permitted
For Cause: Permitted
Post Accident: Permitted
MRO: None required

Wyoming:

Pre Employment: Permitted
Random: Permitted
For Cause: Permitted
Post Accident: Permitted
MRO: None required

SOME CRITICAL DEFINITIONS

ADJUDICATION: The legal process by which a case or claim is settled. May also be the final pronouncement of judgment in a case or claim.

ARREST: The taking of an individual into custody by law enforcement personnel in order to potentially charge the person with an illegal act.

CONVICTION: Verdict of guilty in criminal trial.

DEFERRED ADJUDICATION: The final judgment is delayed. It is likened to probation before a final verdict. Charges are usually dropped and the case is dismissed. During the probation period the disposition is not necessarily considered a conviction. (see Texas Law)

DISMISSAL: Disposing without further consideration. May result in lack of prosecution. Paramount to forgiveness of the crime.

DISPOSITION: The final outcome after plea bargaining, court or trial which may result in a conviction or dismissal.

DIVERSION: Court direction calling for a defendant who was found guilty to enter into a work, educational, or drug rehabilitation program as part of probation. If the conditions of the program are met, charge may be considered a non-conviction.

EXPUNGEMENT: To destroy or erase. Record may or not appear in a criminal history. If record appears, it is noted as "expunged". Record may be destroyed or sealed after a certain period of time. Expunged records are paramount to total forgiveness and erasure of existence.

FELONY: A serious offence whereby punishment is generally in state prison with incarceration for more than one year up to death by execution.

INFRACTION: A violation of a rule or law that is not punishable by incarceration. It is usually a violation of a local ordinance or a traffic offense resulting in a fine.

JUDGMENT: Final decision of the court.

JAIL: A place of confinement that is more than a police station lockup and less than a prison. It is usually used to hold persons either convicted of misdemeanors (minor crimes) or persons awaiting trial or as a lockup for intoxicated and disorderly persons.

MISDEMEANOR: A lesser offense than a felony where punishment is less than a year in jail, possibly a fine, and possible only probation. Generally the conviction does not cause the person to go to prison.

NOLO CONTENDRE: Latin whereby defendant does not contest. Has the legal affect of pleading "guilty".

PRISON: A state or federal correctional institution for incarceration of felony offenders for terms of one year or more. Used synonymously with penitentiary to designate institutions for the imprisonment of persons convicted of the more serious crimes as distinguished from reformatories and county or city jails.

PROBATION: Relief of all or part of a sentence with proper conduct on the part of the person.

QUASH: No prosecution; however there is an option to reopen the case.

VERDICT: Final and formal decision or finding by judge or jury.

For further legal definitions consult Black's Law Dictionary® or review
http://www.legal-definitions.com/

GUIDE FOR DEVELOPING AN APPLICATION FOR EMPLOYMENT
U.S. Equal Employment Opportunity Commission
New Orleans District Office

701 Loyola Avenue, Suite 600
New Orleans, LA 70113-9936
www.eeoc.gov

1-800-669-4000
504-589-2329
504-589-6861 Fax

SEX AND RACE/NATIONAL ORIGIN IDENTIFICATION, HAIR COLOR, EYE COLOR

In order to complete EEO-1 Reports, employers may record information regarding sex, race, and national origin by visual survey of the work force or by maintaining post-employment offer records. Such records should be kept separately from the employee's basic personnel form or other records available to those responsible for personnel decisions. 29 C.F.R.§1602.13. Self-identification is the preferred method of obtaining the information. Individuals cannot be forced to identify themselves by race, sex, or national origin unless required as part of valid affirmative action or Indian preference plan. EEOC Compliance Manual §632.3 (b)(2)(iii).

Although pre-employment inquiries or application coding regarding race and national origin are not per-se violations of Title VII, they may be evidence of discriminatory intent. Dec. No. 75-S-068 (Nov 14, 1974), 1983 EEOC Dec [CCH] ¶6522. Where certain protected groups are absent from an employer's work force, pre-employment inquiries and application coding are evidence of discriminatory intent. Dec No. 72-0455 (Sep 15, 1971), 1973 EEOC Dec. [CCH] ¶ 6306. Pre-employment inquiries as to sex are permissible if made in good faith for a nondiscriminatory purpose. 29 C.F.R. §1604.7

DATE OF BIRTH

A request for date of birth or age is not a per se violation of the ADEA but employment applications that request such information are closely scrutinized to insure that the request is for a permissible purpose. If the application contains this request, it should also have a notice concerning the ADEA 29 C.F.R. §1625.5 The Commission requires employers to maintain records containing employee, but not applicant, date of birth.

29 C.F.R. §1627.3(a). This question on an application form would be evidence that the employer was aware of an applicant's age. Other evidence of discrimination would be required to bring a systemic charge.

HEIGHT/WEIGHT

Minimum height and minimum/maximum weight requirements may have disparate impact on the bases of sex and national origin. EEOC Compliance Manual §621; 29 C.F.R. §1606.6(a)(2).

COPY OF DRIVER'S LICENSE OR OTHER PHOTO IDENTIFICATION

Requiring applicants to include a copy of photo identification provides a mechanism for discriminating on bases of age, race, and national origin.

MARITAL STATUS, NUMBER OF CHILDREN

An employer's or employment agency's inquiry regarding an applicant's marital status coupled with an inquiry about number of children, may provide evidence of discrimination against married women prohibited at 29 C.F.R. §1604.4(a).

CITIZENSHIP STATUS

A citizenship requirement may be discriminatory against members of national origin groups under represented in the employer's work force. EEOC Compliance Manual §622.2(a); 29C.F.R. §1606.5 requiring non-citizens to provide a copy of their visa or work permit may facilitate discrimination on the bases of national origin, race, and or color. Employers cannot specify which documents they will accept from an employee.

ARREST/CHARGE/CONVICTION

Exclusion of individuals on the basis of a conviction record has an adverse impact on African Americans and Hispanics. EEOC Compliance Manual Appendix 604-A.

FOREIGN LANGUAGE FLUENCY

A language fluency requirement may have an adverse impact on members of national origin groups that have native languages other than the required language. EEOC Compliance Manual §623.9(b).

PHYSICAL RECORD

The Americans with Disabilities Act of 1990 prohibits covered entities from conducting a pre-employment medical examination or making inquiries of an applicant as to whether the applicant is an individual with a disability or as to the nature of the disability. 42 U.S.C. §12112(d)(2)(a); 29 C.F.R. §1630.13(a).

PLEASE DESCRIBE ANY ACCOMMODATION (S) YOU REQUIRE TO PERFORM THE ESSENTIAL JOB FUNCTIONS.

This question would require the applicant to reveal a disability in order to adequately answer the question.

The ADA Technical Assistance Manual lists a number of questions that may not be asked on application forms or in job interviews. These include pre-employment questions about illness, use of prescription drugs, and treatment for drug or alcohol addiction. An employer may not ask about an applicant's workers' compensation history in the pre-offer stage, but may obtain such information after making a conditional job offer. The answers to questions about an applicant's workers' compensation history may reveal the existence of a disability. *ADA Technical Assistance Manual*

LIST ANY PHYSICAL OR MENTAL DEFECTS

Pre-employment examinations or inquiries are prohibited by the ADA. 29 C.F.R. §1630.13.

DO YOU LIVE WITH OR PROVIDE CARE FOR ANYONE WHO HAS OR HAD A SERIOUS ILLNESS IN THE PAST FIVE YEARS?
This question would allow an employer to discriminate against the applicant on the basis of relationship or association with a person with a disability 42. U.S.C. §12112(b)(4); 29 C.F.R. §1630.8.

APPLICANT'S CERTIFICATION AND AGREEMENT

Asking for a waiver of the applicant's right under the ADA to not be subject to a pre-employment offer physical examination is not valid and an employer could not require a pre-employment offer physical examination.

An agreement to arbitrate only limits the litigation forum and does not preclude an individual's right to file a charge and have the case investigated by EEOC and does not limit EEOC in bringing actions seeking class-wide and equitable relief. A valid arbitration agreement should follow the Federal Arbitration Act Guidelines, which serve to protect plaintiffs' rights. Gilmer V. Interstate/Johnson Lane Corp., 111 S. Ct. 1647 (1991). This agreement would not be enforceable because it is not part of a valid contract.

The Older Workers Benefits Protection Act of 1990 sets out threshold requirements for valid waivers of rights under the ADEA. 29 U.S.C. §626(0(1).

REMARKS

This calls for subjective evaluations (neatness, personality, character, etc.) that may facilitate discrimination.

EQUAL OPPORTUNITY EMPLOYER

Including this phrase does not negate previous discriminatory questions.

A Summary of Your Rights Under the Fair Credit Reporting Act

The federal Fair Credit Reporting Act (FCRA) promotes the accuracy, fairness, and privacy of information in the files of consumer reporting agencies. There are many types of consumer reporting agencies, including credit bureaus and specialty agencies (such as agencies that sell information about check writing histories, medical records, and rental history records). Here is a summary of your major rights under the FCRA. **For more information, including information about additional rights, go to** *www.ftc.gov/credit* **or write to: Consumer Response Center, Room 130-A, Federal Trade Commission, 600 Pennsylvania Ave. N.W., Washington, D.C. 20580.**

- **You must be told if information in your file has been used against you.** Anyone who uses a credit report or another type of consumer report to deny your application for credit, insurance, or employment - or to take another adverse action against you - must tell you, and must give you the name, address, and phone number of the agency that provided the information.
- **You have the right to know what is in your file.** You may request and obtain all the information about you in the files of a consumer reporting agency (your "file disclosure"). You will be required to provide proper identification, which may include your Social Security number. In many cases, the disclosure will be free. You are entitled to a free file disclosure if:
  - a person has taken adverse action against you because of information in your credit report;
  - you are the victim of identify theft and place a fraud alert in your file;
  - your file contains inaccurate information as a result of fraud;
  - you are on public assistance;
  - you are unemployed but expect to apply for employment within 60 days.

In addition, by September 2005 all consumers will be entitled to one free disclosure every 12 months upon request from each nationwide credit bureau and from nationwide specialty consumer reporting agencies. See *www.ftc.gov/credit* for additional information.

- **You have the right to ask for a credit score.** Credit scores are numerical summaries of your credit-worthiness based on information from credit bureaus. You may request a credit score from consumer reporting agencies that create scores or distribute scores used in residential real property loans, but you will have to pay for it. In some mortgage transactions, you will receive credit score information for free from the mortgage lender.
- **You have the right to dispute incomplete or inaccurate information.** If you identify information in your file that is incomplete or inaccurate, and report it to the consumer reporting agency, the agency must investigate unless your dispute is frivolous See *www.ftc.gov/credit* for an explanation of dispute procedures.

- **Consumer reporting agencies must correct or delete inaccurate, incomplete, or unverifiable information.** Inaccurate, incomplete or unverifiable information must be removed or corrected, usually within 30 days. However, a consumer reporting

- **Consumer reporting agencies may not report outdated negative information.** In most cases, a consumer reporting agency may not report negative information that is more than seven years old, or bankruptcies that are more than 10 years old.

- **Access to your file is limited.** A consumer reporting agency may provide information about you only to people with a valid need—usually to consider an application with a creditor, insurer, employer, landlord, or other business. The FCRA specifies those with a valid need for access.

- **You must give your consent for reports to be provided to employers.** A consumer reporting agency may not give out information about you to your employer, or a potential employer, without your written consent given to the employer. Written consent generally is not required in the trucking industry. For more information, go to *www.ftc.gov/credit*.

- **You may limit "prescreened" offers of credit and insurance you get based on information in your credit report.** Unsolicited "prescreened" offers for credit and insurance must include a toll-free phone number you can call if you choose to remove your name and address from the lists these offers are based on. You may opt-out with the nationwide credit bureaus at 1-888-5-OPTOUT (1-888-567-8688).

- **You may seek damages from violators.** If a consumer reporting agency, or, in some cases, a user of consumer reports or a furnisher of information to a consumer reporting agency violates the FCRA, you may be able to sue in state or federal court.

- **Identity theft victims and active duty military personnel have additional rights.** For more information, visit *www.ftc.gov/credit*.

States may enforce the FCRA, and many states have their own consumer reporting laws. In some cases, you may have more rights under state law. For more information, contact your state or local consumer protection agency or your state Attorney General. Federal enforcers are:

TYPE OF BUSINESS	CONTACT
Consumer reporting agencies, creditors and others not listed below	Federal Trade Commission: Consumer Response Center—FCRA Washington, DC 20580 1-877-382-4357
National banks, federal branches/agencies of foreign banks (word "National" or initials "N.A." appear in or after bank's name)	Office of the Comptroller of the Currency Compliance Management, Mail Stop 6-6 Washington, DC 20219 1-800-613-6743
Federal Reserve System member banks (except national banks, and federal branches/ agencies of foreign banks)	Federal Reserve Board Division of Consumer & Community Affairs Washington, DC 20551 1-202-452-3693
Savings associations and federally chartered savings banks (word "Federal" or initials "F.S.B." appear in federal institution's name)	Office of Thrift Supervision Consumer Complaints Washington, DC 20552 1-800-842-6929
Federal credit units (words "Federal Credit Union" appear in institution's name)	National Credit Union Administration 1775 Duke Street Alexandria, VA 22314 1-703-519-4600
State-chartered banks that are not members of the Federal Reserve System	Federal Deposit Insurance Corporation Consumer Response Center, 2345 Grand Avenue, Suite 100 Kansas City, MO 64108-2638 1-877-275-3342
Air, surface, or rail common carriers regulated by former Civil Aeronautics Board or Interstate Commerce Commission	Department of Transportation, Office of Financial Management Washington, DC 20590 1-202-366-1306
Activities subject to the Packers and Stockyards Act, 1921	Department of Agriculture Office of Deputy Administrator—GIPSA Washington, DC 20250 1-202-720-7051

Un Resumen de Sus Derechos en Virtud de la Ley de Informe Justo de Crédito

La Ley Federal de Informe Justo de Crédito *(Fair Credit Reporting Act, FCRA)* fomenta la exactitud, justicia y privacidad de la información en los expedientes de las agencias de informe del consumidor. Existen muchos tipos de agencias de informe del consumidor, incluyendo las agencias de crédito (credit bureaus) y las especializadas (como agencias que venden información sobre historial de firma de cheques, expedientes médicos e historial de alquiler). A continuación tiene un breve **resumen de sus principales derechos en virtud de la FCRA. Para más información, incluyendo información sobre derechos adicionales, visite www.ftc.gov/credit/espanol_loans.htm o escriba a: Consumer Response Center, Room 130- A, Federal Trade Commission, 600 Pennsylvania Ave. N.W., Washington, D.C. 20580.**

- **Deben notificarle si la información en su expediente se ha utilizado en contra de usted.** Todo aquel que utilice un informe de crédito u otro tipo de informe de consumidor para denegar su solicitud de crédito, seguro o empleo, o para emprender otra acción contra usted, debe informarle y debe darle el nombre, la dirección y el teléfono de la agencia que proporcionó esa información.
- **Tiene derecho a saber lo que está en su expediente.** Puede solicitar y obtener toda la información sobre usted en los archivos de una agencia de informe del consumidor. Deberá proporcionar identificación, que puede incluir su número de Seguro Social. En muchos casos, la divulgación de esta información será gratuita. Tiene derecho a una divulgación gratuita si:
  - una persona ha emprendido una acción adversa contra usted debido a información en su informe de crédito;
  - usted es víctima de un robo de identidad y se coloca una alerta de fraude en su expediente;
  - su expediente contiene información no exacta como resultado de fraude;
  - usted recibe asistencia pública;
  - no está empleado pero anticipa solicitar empleo en 60 días.

Asimismo, para septiembre de 2005, todos los consumidores tendrán derecho a una divulgación cada 12 meses si así lo solicitan a cada agencia de crédito nacional y de las agencias nacionales de informe del consumidor especializadas. Para información adicional, visite *www.ftc.gov/credit/espanol_loans.htm.*

- **Tiene derecho a pedir su puntuación de crédito.** Las puntuaciones de crédito son resúmenes numéricos de su valía de crédito basados en información de las agencias de crédito. Puede solicitar una puntuación de crédito de agencias de informe del consumidor que crean puntuaciones o distribuyen las puntuaciones utilizadas en préstamos de bienes raíces residenciales, pero tendrá que pagar para recibirla. En algunas transacciones hipotecarias, el prestamista le dará gratuitamente información sobre su puntuación de crédito.

- **Tiene derecho a confrontar información incompleta o no exacta.** Si identifica información en su expediente que es incompleta o inexacta, y la reporta a la agencia de informe del consumidor, la agencia debe investigar a menos que su confrontación sea frívola. Visite *www.ftc.gov/credit/espanol_loans.htm* para una explicación de los procedimientos de confrontación.
- **Las agencias de informe del consumidor deben corregir o eliminar información inexacta, incompleta o no verificable.** La información no exacta, incompleta o no verificable debe ser retirada o corregida, generalmente dentro de 30 días. No obstante, una agencia de informe del consumidor puede seguir reportando información si ha verificado su exactitud.
- **Las agencias de informe del consumidor no pueden reportar información negativa atrasada.** En la mayoría de los casos, una agencia de informe del consumidor puede no reportar información negativa ocurrida hace más de siete años, ni quiebras ocurridas hace más de 10 años.
- **El acceso a su expediente es limitado.** Una agencia de informe del consumidor puede proporcionar información sobre usted solamente a personas que realmente la necesiten—generalmente para considerar una solicitud con un acreedor, asegurador, empleador, propietario de vivienda u otro negocio. La FCRA especifica quiénes son las personas que tienen una necesidad válida de acceso.
- **Debe otorgar su consentimiento para que se envíen sus informes a empleadores.** Una agencia de informe del consumidor no puede dar información sobre usted a su empleador, o a un posible empleador, sin su consentimiento escrito previo otorgado al empleador. El consentimiento escrito generalmente no es requerido en la industria de camiones. Para más información visite *www.ftc.gov/credit/espanol_loans.htm.*
- **Puede limitar las ofertas "preevaluadas" de crédito y seguro que obtiene basadas en información en su informe de crédito.** Las ofertas "preevaluadas" de crédito y seguro deben incluir un número de teléfono sin cargo al que puede llamar si desea eliminar su nombre y dirección de las listas en las que se basan estas ofertas. Puede optar por no figurar en las listas de las agencias de crédito llamando al 1-888-5 OPTOUT (1-888-567-8888).
- **Puede obtener compensación de los acreedores.** Si una agencia de informe del consumidor, o en algunos casos, un usuario de informes de consumidor o proveedor de información a una agencia de informe del consumidor infringe la FCRA, usted puede presentar un pleito en un tribunal estatal o federal.
- **Las víctimas de robo de identidad y el personal militar en activo tienen derechos adicionales.** Para más información, visite *www.ftc.gov/credit/espanol_loans.htm.*

Los estados tienen autoridad para hacer cumplir la FCRA, y muchos estados tienen su propia legislación de informe del consumidor. En algunos casos, usted puede tener más derechos en virtud de la ley estatal. Comuníquese con su agencia de protección estatal o local del consumidor o su Fiscal general estatal. Las agencias a nivel federal son:

TIPO DE NEGOCIO	CONTACTAR
Agencias de informe del consumidor, acreedores y otros no mencionados abajo	Federal Trade Commission: Consumer Response Center—FCRA Washington, DC 20580 1-877-382-4357
Bancos nacionales, sucursales/agencias federales de bancos extranjeros (con la palabra "National" o las iniciales "N.A." en o después del nombre del banco)	Office of the Comptroller of the Currency Compliance Management, Mail Stop 6-6 Washington, DC 20219 1-800-613-6743
Bancos que pertenecen al Sistema de la Reserva Federal (salvo bancos nacionales, y sucursales/agencias federales de bancos extranjeros)	Federal Reserve Board Division of Consumer & Community Affairs Washington, DC 20551 1-202-452-3693
Asociaciones de ahorros y cajas de ahorros con acreditación federal (con la palabra "Federal" o las iniciales "F.S.B." en el nombre de la institución federal)	Office of Thrift Supervision Consumer Complaints Washington, DC 20552 1-800-842-6929
Bancos de crédito federales (con las palabras "Federal Credit Union" en el nombre de la institución)	National Credit Union Administration 1775 Duke Street Alexandria, VA 22314 1-703-519-4600
Bancos acreditados a nivel estatal que no son miembros del Sistema de la Reserva Federal	Federal Deposit Insurance Corporation Consumer Response Center, 2345 Grand Avenue, Suite 100 Kansas City, MO 64108-2638 1-877-275-3342
Transportadores por aire, superficie o ferrocarril regulados por la antigue Junta de Aeronáutica Civil o por la Comisión Interestatal de Comercio	Department of Transportation, Office of Financial Management Washington, DC 20590 1-202-366-1306
Actividades sujetas a la Ley de Empacadores y Estibadores de 1921	Department of Agriculture Office of Deputy Administrator—GIPSA Washington, DC 20250 1-202-720-7051

All users subject to the Federal Trade Commission's jurisdiction must comply with all applicable regulations, including regulations promulgated after this notice was prescribed in 2004. Information about applicable regulations currently in effect can be found at the Commission's Web site, *www.ftc.gov/credit*. Persons not subject to the Commission's jurisdiction should consult with their regulators to find any relevant regulation

NOTICE TO USERS OF CONSUMER REPORTS: OBLIGATIONS OF USERS UNDER THE FCRA

The Fair Credit Reporting Act (FCRA), 15 U.S.C. 1681-1681y, requires that this notice be provided to inform users of consumer reports of their legal obligations. State law may impose additional requirements. The text of the FCRA is set forth in full at the Federal Trade Commission's Website at *www.ftc.gov/credit*. At the end of this document is a list of United States Code citations for the FCRA. Other information about user duties is also available at the Commission's Web site. **Users must consult the relevant provisions of the FCRA for details about their obligations under the FCRA**.

The first section of this summary sets forth the responsibilities imposed by the FCRA on all users of consumer reports. The subsequent sections discuss the duties of users of reports that contain specific types of information, or that are used for certain purposes, and the legal consequences of violations. If you are a furnisher of information to a consumer reporting agency (CRA), you have additional obligations and will receive a separate notice from the CRA describing your duties as a furnisher.

I. OBLIGATIONS OF ALL USERS OF CONSUMER REPORTS

A. Users Must Have a Permissible Purpose

Congress has limited the use of consumer reports to protect consumers, privacy. All users must have a permissible purpose under the FCRA to obtain a consumer report. Section 604 contains a list of the permissible purposes under the law. These are:

- As ordered by a court or a federal grand jury subpoena. *Section 604(a)(1)*
- As instructed by the consumer in writing. *Section 604(a)(2)*
- For the extension of credit as a result of an application from a consumer, or the review or collection of a consumer's account. *Section 604(a)(3)(A)*
- For employment purposes, including hiring and promotion decisions, where the consumer has given written permission. *Sections 604(a)(3)(B) and 604(b)*
- For the underwriting of insurance as a result of an application from a consumer. *Section 604(a)(3)(C)*

- When there is a legitimate business need, in connection with a business transaction that is initiated by the consumer. *Section 604(a)(3)(F)(i)*
- To review a consumer's account to determine whether the consumer continues to meet the terms of the account. Section *604(a)(3)(F)(ii)*
- To determine a consumer's eligibility for a license or other benefit granted by a governmental instrumentality required by law to consider an applicant's financial responsibility or status. Section *604(a)(3)(D)*
- For use by a potential investor or servicer, or current insurer, in a valuation or assessment of the credit or prepayment risks associated with an existing credit obligation. *Section 604(a)(3)(E)*
- For use by state and local officials in connection with the determination of child support payments, or modifications and enforcement thereof. *Sections 604(a)(4 and 604(a)(5)*

In addition, creditors and insurers may obtain certain consumer re port information for the purpose of making "prescreened" unsolicited offers of credit or insurance. *Section 604(c)*. The particular obligations of users of "prescreened" information are described in Section VII below.

B. Users Must Provide Certifications

Section 604(f) prohibits any person from obtaining a consumer report from a consumer reporting agency (CRA) unless the person has certified to the CRA the permissible purpose(s) for which the report is being obtained and certifies that the report will not be used for any other purpose.

C. Users Must Notify Consumers When Adverse Actions Are Taken

The term "adverse action" is defined very broadly by Section 603. "Adverse actions" include all business, credit, and employment actions affecting consumers that can be considered to have a negative impact as defined by Section 603(k) of the FCRA—such as denying or canceling credit or insurance, or denying employment or promotion. No adverse action occurs in a credit transaction where the creditor makes a counteroffer that is accepted by the consumer.

1. Adverse Actions Based on Information Obtained From a CRA

If a user takes any type of adverse action as defined by the FCRA that is based at least in part on information contained in a consumer report, Section 615(a) requires the user to notify the consumer. The notification may be done in writing, orally, or by electronic means. It must include the following:

- The name, address, and telephone number of the CRA (including a toll-free telephone number, if it is a nationwide CRA) that provided the report.

- A statement that the CRA did not make the adverse decision and is not able to explain why the decision was made.
- A statement setting forth the consumer's right to obtain a free disclosure of the consumer's file from the CRA if the consumer makes a request within 60 days.
- A statement setting forth the consumer's right to dispute directly with the CRA the accuracy or completeness of any information provided by the CRA.

2. Adverse Actions Based on Information Obtained From Third Parties Who Are Not Consumer Reporting Agencies

If a person denies (or increases the charge for) credit for personal, family, or household purposes based either wholly or partly upon information from a person other than a CRA, and the information is the type of consumer information covered by the FCRA, Section 615(b)(1) requires that the user clearly and accurately disclose to the consumer his or her right to be told the nature of the information that was relied upon if the consumer makes a written request within 60 days of notification. The user must provide the disclosure within a reasonable period of time following the consumer's written request.

3. Adverse Actions Based on Information Obtained From Affiliates

If a person takes an adverse action involving insurance, employment, or a credit transaction initiated by the consumer, based on information of the type covered by the FCRA, and this information was obtained from an entity affiliated with the user of the information by common ownership or control, Section 615(b)(2) requires the user to notify the consumer of the adverse action. The notice must inform the consumer that he or she may obtain a disclosure of the nature of the information relied upon by making a written request within 60 days of receiving the adverse action notice. If the consumer makes such a request, the user must disclose the nature of the information not later than 30 days after receiving the request. If consumer report information is shared among affiliates and then used for an adverse action, the user must make an adverse action disclosure as set forth in I.C. 1 above.

D. Users Have-Obligations When Fraud and Active Duty Military Alerts are in Files

When a consumer has placed a fraud alert, including one relating to identity theft, or an active duty military alert with a nationwide consumer reporting agency as defined in Section 603(p) and resellers, Section 605A(h) imposes limitations on users of reports obtained from the consumer reporting agency in certain circumstances, including the establishment of a new credit plan and the issuance of additional credit cards. For initial fraud alerts and active duty alerts, the user must have reasonable policies and procedures in place to form a belief that the user knows the identity of the applicant or contact the consumer at a telephone number specified by the consumer; in the case of extended fraud alerts, the user must contact the consumer in accordance with the contact information provided in the consumer's alert.

E. *Users Have Obligations When Notified of an Address Discrepancy*

Section 605(h) requires nationwide CRAs, as defined in Section 603(p), to notify users that request reports when the address for a consumer provided by the user in requesting the report is substantially different from the addresses in the consumer's file. When this occurs, users must comply with regulations specifying the procedures to be followed, which will be issued by the Federal Trade Commission and the banking and credit union regulators. The Federal Trade Commission's regulations will be available at *www.ftc.gov/credit.*

F. *Users Have Obligations When Disposing of Records*

Section 628 requires that all users of consumer report information have in place procedures to properly dispose of records containing this information. The Federal Trade Commission, the Securities and Exchange Commission, and the banking and credit union regulators have issued regulations covering disposal. The Federal Trade Commission's regulations maybe found at *www.ftc.gov/credit.*

II. CREDITORS MUST MAKE ADDITIONAL DISCLOSURES

If a person uses a consumer report in connection with an application for, or a grant, extension, or provision of, credit to a consumer on material terms that are materially less favorable than the most favorable terms available to a substantial proportion of consumers from or through that person, based in whole or in part on a consumer report, the person must provide a risk-based pricing notice to the consumer in accordance with regulations to be jointly prescribed by the Federal Trade Commission and the Federal Reserve Board.

Section 609(g) requires a disclosure by all persons that make or arrange loans secured by residential real property (one to four units) and that use credit scores. These persons must provide credit scores and other information about credit scores to applicants, including the disclosure set forth in Section 609(g)(1)(D) ("Notice to the Home Loan Applicant").

III. OBLIGATIONS OF USERS WHEN CONSUMER REPORTS ARE OBTAINED FOR EMPLOYMENT PURPOSES

A. *Employment Other Than in the Trucking Industry*

If information from a CRA is used for employment purposes, the user has specific duties, which are set forth in Section 604(b) of the FCRA. The user must:

- Make a clear and conspicuous written disclosure to the consumer before the report is obtained, in a document that consists solely of the disclosure, that a consumer report may be obtained.
- Obtain from the consumer prior written authorization. Authorization to access reports during the term of employment may be obtained at the time of employment

- Certify to the CRA that the above steps have been followed, that the information being obtained will not be used in violation of any federal or state equal opportunity law or regulation, and that, if any adverse action is to be taken based on the consumer report, a copy of the report and a summary of the consumer's rights will be provided to the consumer.
- Before taking an adverse action, the user must provide a copy of the report to the consumer as well as the summary of consumer's rights. (The user should receive this summary from the CRA.) A Section 615(a) adverse action notice should be sent after the adverse action is taken.

An adverse action notice also is required in employment situations if credit information (other than transactions and experience data) obtained from an affiliate is used to deny employment. Section 615(b)(2)

The procedures for investigative consumer reports and employee misconduct investigations are set forth below.

B. Employment in the Trucking Industry

Special rules apply for truck drivers where the only interaction between the consumer and the potential employer is by mail, telephone, or computer. In this case, the consumer may provide consent orally or electronically, and an adverse action may be made orally, in writing, or electronically. The consumer may obtain a copy of any report relied upon by the trucking company by contacting the company.

IV. OBLIGATIONS WHEN INVESTIGATIVE CONSUMER REPORTS ARE USED

Investigative consumer reports are a special type of consumer report in which information about a consumer's character, general reputation, personal characteristics, and mode of living is obtained through personal interviews by an entity or person that is a consumer reporting agency. Consumers who are the subjects of such reports are given special rights under the FCRA. If a user intends to obtain an investigative consumer report, Section 606 requires the following:

- The user must disclose to the consumer that an investigative consumer report may be obtained. This must be done in a written disclosure that is mailed, or otherwise delivered, to the consumer at some time before or not later than three days after the date on which the report was first requested. The disclosure must include a statement informing the consumer of his or her right to request additional disclosures of the nature and scope of the investigation as described below, and the summary of consumer rights required by Section 609 of the FCRA. (The summary of consumer rights will be provided by the CRA that conducts the investigation.)

- The user must certify to the CRA that the disclosures set forth above have been made and that the user will make the disclosure described below.
- Upon the written request of a consumer made within a reasonable period of time after the disclosures required above, the user must make a complete disclosure of the nature and scope of the investigation. This must be made in a written statement that is mailed, or otherwise delivered, to the consumer no later than five days after the date on *which the* request was received from the consumer or the report was first requested, whichever is later in time.

V. SPECIAL PROCEDURES FOR EMPLOYEE INVESTIGATIONS

Section 603(x) provides special procedures for investigations of suspected misconduct by an employee or for compliance with Federal, state or local laws and regulations or the rules of a self-regulatory organization, and compliance with written policies of the employer. These investigations are not treated as consumer reports so long as the employer or its agent complies with the procedures set forth in Section 603(x), and a summary describing the nature and scope of the inquiry is made to the employee if an adverse action is taken based on the investigation.

VI. OBLIGATIONS OF USERS OF MEDICAL INFORMATION

Section 604(g) limits the use of medical information obtained from consumer reporting agencies (other than payment information that appears in a coded form that does not identify the medical provider). If the information is to be used for an insurance transaction, the consumer must give consent to the user of the report or the information must be coded. If the report is to be used for employment purposes - or in connection with a credit transaction (except as provided in regulations issued by the banking and credit union regulators)—the consumer must provide specific written consent and the medical information must be relevant. Any user who receives medical information shall not disclose the information to any other person (except where necessary to carry out the purpose for which the information was disclosed, or as permitted by statute, regulation, or order).

VII. OBLIGATIONS OF USERS OF "PRESCREENED" LISTS

The FCRA permits creditors and insurers to obtain limited consumer report information for use in connection with unsolicited offers of credit or insurance under certain circumstances. Sections 603(1), 604(c), and 615(d). This practice is known as "prescreening" and typically involves obtaining from a CRA a list of consumers who meet certain preestablished criteria. If any person intends to use prescreened lists, that person must (1) before the offer is made, establish the criteria that will be relied upon to make the offer and to grant credit or insurance, and (2) maintain such criteria on Me for a three-year period beginning on the date on which the offer is made to each consumer. In addition, any user must provide with each written solicitation a clear and conspicuous statement that:

- Information contained in a consumer's CRA file was used in connection with the transaction.
- The consumer received the offer because he or she satisfied the criteria for credit worthiness or insurability used to screen for the offer.
- Credit or insurance may not be extended if, after the consumer responds, it is determined that the consumer does not meet the criteria used for screening or any applicable criteria bearing on credit worthiness or insurability, or the consumer does not furnish required collateral.
- The consumer may prohibit the use of information in his or her file in connection with future prescreened offers of credit or insurance by contacting the notification system established by the CRA that provided the report. The statement must include the address and toll-free telephone number of the appropriate notification system.

In addition, once the Federal Trade Commission by rule has established the format, type size, and manner of the disclosure required by Section 615(d), users must be in compliance with the rule. The FTC's regulations will be at *www.ftc.gov/credit.*

VIII. OBLIGATIONS OF RESELLERS

A. Disclosure and Certification Requirements

Section 607(e) requires any person who obtains a consumer report for resale to take the following steps:

- Disclose the identity of the end-user to the source CRA.
- Identify to the source CRA each permissible purpose for which the report will be furnished to the end-user.
- Establish and follow reasonable procedures to ensure that reports are resold only for permissible purposes, including procedures to obtain:
    (1) the identity of all end-users;
    (2) certifications from all users of each purpose for which reports will be used; and
    (3) certifications that reports will not be used for any purpose other than the purpose(s) specified to the reseller. Resellers must make reasonable efforts to verify this information before selling the report.

B. Reinvestigations by Resellers

Under Section 611(f), if a consumer disputes the accuracy or completeness of information in a report prepared by a reseller, the reseller must determine whether this is a result of an action or omission on its part and, if so, correct or delete the information. If not, the reseller must send the dispute to the source CRA for reinvestigation. When any CRA notifies the reseller of the results of an investigation, the reseller must immediately convey the information to the consumer.

C. Fraud Alerts and Resellers

Section 605A(f) requires resellers who receive fraud alerts or active duty alerts from another consumer reporting agency to include these in their reports.

IX. LIABILITY FOR VIOLATIONS OF THE FCRA

Failure to comply with the FCRA can result in state government or federal government enforcement actions, as well as private lawsuits. *Sections 616, 617, and 621.* In addition, any person who knowingly and willfully obtains a consumer report under false pretenses may face criminal prosecution. *Section 619.*

> All furnishers subject to the Federal Trade Commission's jurisdiction must comply with all applicable regulations, including regulations promulgated after this notice was prescribed in 2004. Information about applicable regulations currently in effect can be found at the Commission's Web site, *www.ftc.gov/credit*. Furnishers who are not subject to the Commission's jurisdiction should consult with their regulators to rind any relevant regulations.

NOTICE TO FURNISHERS OF INFORMATION: OBLIGATIONS OF FURNISHERS UNDER THE FCRA

The federal Fair Credit Reporting Act (FCRA), 15 U. S.C. 1681-1681y, imposes responsibilities on all persons who famish information to consumer reporting agencies (CRAs). These responsibilities are found in Section 623 of the FCRA, 15 U.S.C. 168 1s-2. State law may impose additional requirements on furnishers. All furnishers of information to CRAs should become familiar with the applicable laws and may want to consult with their counsel to ensure that they are in compliance. The text of the FCRA is set forth in full at the Website of the Federal Trade Commission (FTC): *www.ftc.gov/credit*. A list of the sections of the FCRA cross referenced to the U.S. Code is at the end of this document.

Section 623 imposes the following duties upon furnishers:

Accuracy Guidelines

The banking and credit union regulators and the FTC will promulgate guidelines and regulations dealing with the accuracy of information provided to CRAs by furnishers. The regulations and guidelines issued by the FTC will be available at *www.ftc.gov/credit* when they are issued. *Section 623(e).*

General Prohibition on Reporting Inaccurate Information

The FCRA prohibits information furnishers from providing information to a CRA that they know or have reasonable cause to believe is inaccurate. However, the furnisher is not subject to this general prohibition if it clearly and conspicuously specifies an address to which consumers may write to notify the furnisher that certain information is inaccurate. *Sections 623(a)(1)(A)* and *(a)(1)(C).*

Duty to Correct and Update Information

If at any time a person who regularly and in the ordinary course of business furnishes information to one or more CRAs determines that the information provided is not complete or accurate, the furnisher must promptly provide complete and accurate information to the CRA. In addition, the furnisher must notify all CRAs that received the information of any corrections, and must thereafter report only the complete and accurate information. *Section 623(a)(2).*

Duties After Notice of Dispute from Consumer

If a consumer notifies a furnisher, at an address specified for the furnisher for such notices, that specific information is inaccurate, and the information is, in fact, inaccurate, the furnisher must thereafter report the correct information to CRAs. *Section 623(a)(1)(B).*

If a, consumer notifies a furnisher that the consumer disputes the completeness or accuracy of any information reported by the furnisher, the furnisher may not subsequently report that information to a CRA without providing notice of the dispute. *Section 623(a)(3).*

The federal banking and credit union regulators and the FTC will issue regulations that will identify when an information furnisher must investigate a dispute made directly to the furnisher by a consumer. Once these regulations are issued, furnishers must comply with them and complete an investigation within 30 days (or 45 days, if the consumer later provides relevant additional information) unless the dispute is frivolous or irrelevant or comes from a "credit repair organization." The FTC regulations will be available at *www.ftc.gov/credit. Section 623(a)(8).*

Duties After Notice of Dispute from Consumer Reporting Agency

If a CRA notifies a furnisher that a consumer disputes the completeness or accuracy of information provided by the furnisher, the furnisher has a duty to follow certain procedures. The furnisher must:

* Conduct an investigation and review all relevant information provided by the CRA including information given to the CRA by the consumer. *Sections 623(b)(1)(A) and (b)(1)(B).*
* Report the results to the CRA that referred the dispute, and, if the investigation establishes that the information was, in fact, incomplete or inaccurate, report the results to all CRAs to which the furnisher provided the information that compile and maintain files on a nationwide basis. *Section 623(b)(1)(C) and*
* Complete the above steps within 30 days from the date the CRA receives the dispute (or 45 days, if the consumer later provides relevant additional information to the CRA). *Section 623(b)(2).*

* Promptly modify or delete the information, or block its reporting. *Section 623(b)(1)(E)*.

Duty to Report Voluntary Closing of Credit Accounts

If a consumer voluntarily closes a credit account, any person who regularly and in the ordinary course of business furnishes information to one or more CRAs must report this fact when it provides information to CRAs for the time period in which the account was closed. *Section 623(a)(4)*.

Duty to Report Dates of Delinquencies

If a furnisher reports information concerning a delinquent account placed for collection, charged to profit or loss, or subject to any similar action, the furnisher must, within 90 days after reporting the information, provide the CRA with the month and the year of the commencement of the delinquency that immediately preceded the action, so that the agency will know how long to keep the information in the consumer's file. *Section 623(a)(5)*.

Any person, such as a debt collector, that has acquired or is responsible for collecting delinquent accounts and that reports information to CRAs may comply with the requirements of Section 623(a)(5) (until there is a consumer dispute) by reporting the same delinquency date previously reported by the creditor. If the creditor did not report this date, they may comply with the FCRA by establishing reasonable procedures to obtain and report delinquency dates, or, if a delinquency date can-not be reasonably obtained, by following reasonable procedures to ensure that the date reported precedes the date when the account was placed for collection, charged to profit or loss, or subjected to any similar action. *Section 623(a) (5)*.

Duties of Financial Institutions When Reporting Negative Information

Financial institutions that furnish information to "nationwide' consumer reporting agencies, as defined in Section 603(p), must notify consumers in writing if they may furnish or have furnished negative information to a CRA. *Section 623(a)(7)*. The Federal Reserve Board has prescribed model disclosures, 12 CFR Part 222, App. B.

Duties When Furnishing Medical Information

A furnisher whose primary business is providing medical services, products, or devices (and such furnisher's agents or assignees) is a medical information furnisher for the purposes of the FCRA and must notify all CRAs to which it reports of this fact. *Section 623(a)(9)*. This notice will enable CRAs to comply with their duties under Section 604(g) when reporting medical information.

Duties When ID Theft Occurs

All furnishers must have in place reasonable procedures to respond to notifications from CRAs that information furnished is the result of identity theft, and to prevent refurnishing the information in the future. A furnisher may not furnish information that a consumer has identified as resulting from identity theft unless the furnisher subsequently knows or is informed by the consumer that the information is correct. *Section 623(a)(6).* If a furnisher learns that it has furnished inaccurate information due to identity theft, it must notify each consumer reporting agency of the correct information and must thereafter report only complete and accurate information *Section 623(a)(2).* When any furnisher of information is notified pursuant to the procedures set forth in Section 605B that a debt has resulted from identity theft, the furnisher may not sell, transfer, or place for collection the debt except in certain limited circumstances. *Section 615(f).*

The FTC's Web site, *www.ftc.gov/credit*, has more information about the FCRA, including publications for businesses and the full text of the FCRA.

Federal Employment Law Summaries

• AMERICANS WITH DISABILITIES ACT OF 1990 (ADA)

What does it do: Title I requires that employers (which includes religious entities) with 15 or more employees provide qualified individuals with disabilities an equal opportunity to benefit from the full range of employment-related opportunities available to others. It prohibits discrimination in recruitment, hiring, promotion, training, pay, social activities, and other privileges of employment.

Monitored—Enforced by: Complaints must be filed with the U.S. Equal Employment Opportunity Commission (EEOC) within 180 days of the date of discrimination, or 300 days if the charge is filed with the designated State or local fair employment practice agency. After a "right-to-sue" letter is received from the EEOC the individual can file a lawsuit in Federal court.

Year enacted/amended: 1990

• AGE DISCRIMINATION IN EMPLOYMENT ACT (ADEA)

What does it do: The Age Discrimination in Employment Act (ADEA) prohibits employment practices that discriminate on the basis of age, unless age is a bona fide occupational qualification, or the practice is based on reasonable factors other than age. It covers employers with 20 or more employees, labor unions with 25 or more members, local and state governments, and employment agencies. ADEA says you can't, among other things, refuse to hire an applicant because he or she is over 40, or force an employee to retire because of age.

Monitored—Enforced by: The Equal Employment Opportunity Commission (EEOC) shall have the power to make investigations and require the keeping of records necessary or appropriate for the administration of this chapter in accordance with the powers and procedures provided.

Year enacted/amended: 1967/1978

• CONSOLIDATED OMNIBUS BUDGET RECONCILIATION ACT (COBRA) —

What does it do? The Consolidated Omnibus Budget Reconciliation Act (COBRA) was designed to permit individuals who would otherwise lose their health insurance coverage to continue coverage through their employer or former employer at group rates if they are willing to pay the full premium themselves. The law requires employers to offer the opportunity to purchase continued group health coverage to four overlapping but distinct groups:

1. Employees and their families who lose coverage because of the employee's termination or reduction in hours.

2. Divorcees, widows, and their children who lose coverage as a result of divorce or the death of an employed spouse.

3. Dependent children who lose coverage because they exceed the plan's age limit for eligibility.

4. Spouses and dependent children who lose group coverage because the covered employee became entitled to Medicare.

COBRA also provides continuation coverage for retired employees and their spouses and children who lose coverage because the employer is involved in bankruptcy proceedings.

Monitored—Enforced by: Departments of Labor and Treasury. The Internal Revenue Service (apart of the Department of Treasury) is responsible for publishing regulations on COBRA provisions relating to eligibility and premiums. The Equal Employment Opportunity Commission (EEOC) shall have the power to make investigations and require the keeping of records necessary or appropriate for the administration of this chapter in accordance with the powers and procedures provided.

Year enacted/amended: 1986

• DRIVER'S PRIVACY PROTECTION ACT (DPPA)

What does the law do? A State department of motor vehicles, and any officer, employee, or contractor, thereof, shall not knowingly disclose or otherwise make available to any person or entity any personal information about any individual obtained by the department in connection with a motor vehicle record.

Monitored—Enforced by: The U.S. Attorney General, State departments of motor vehicles, and any individual whose personal information has knowingly or unknowingly been released/used without permissible use.

Year enacted/amended: 1994/1997

• EQUAL EMPLOYMENT OPPORTUNITY COMMISSION (EEOC)

The EEOC was established by Title VII of the Civil Rights Act of 1964 and began operating on July 2, 1965. With its headquarters in Washington, D.C., and through the operations of 50 field offices nationwide, the EEOC coordinates all federal equal employment opportunity regulations, practices, and policies. The Commission interprets employment discrimination laws, monitors the federal sector employment discrimination program, provides funding and support to state and local Fair Employment Practices Agencies (FEPAs), and sponsors outreach and technical assistance programs.

Monitored—Enforced by: The EEOC enforces the following federal statutes: Title VII of the Civil Rights Act of 1964, as amended, prohibiting employment discrimination on the basis of race, color, religion, sex, or national origin; the Age Discrimination in Employment Act of (ADEA) of 1967, as amended, prohibiting employment discrimination against individuals 40 years of age and older; the Equal Pay Act (EPA) of 1963 prohibiting discrimination on the basis of gender in compensation for substantially similar work under similar conditions. Title I and Title V of the Americans with Disabilities Act (ADA) of 1990, prohibiting employment discrimination on the basis of disability in the private sector and state and local government; Section 501 and 505 of the Rehabilitation Act of 1973, as amended, prohibiting employment discrimination against federal employees with disabilities; and The Civil Rights Act of 1991 providing monetary damages in cases of intentional discrimination and clarifying provisions regarding disparate impact actions.

Year enacted/amended: 1964

• EMPLOYEE POLYGRAPH PROTECTION ACT (EPPA)

What does the law do? Businesses cannot request, suggest or require any job applicant to take a pre-employment polygraph examination. Additionally, businesses can request a current employee to take a polygraph examination or suggest to an employee that a polygraph examination be taken, only when specific conditions have been satisfied. However, the employer cannot require current employees to take the examination, and if an employee refuses a request or suggestion, the employer cannot discipline or discharge the employee based on the refusal to submit to the examination.

Monitored—Enforced by: The Secretary of Labor has the enforcement authority.

Year enacted/amended: 1988

• EMPLOYEE RETIREMENT INCOME SECURITY ACT (ERISA)

What does the law do? The purpose of ERISA is to protect the interests of participants and their beneficiaries in employee benefit plans. The law requires that sponsors of private employee benefit plans provide participants and beneficiaries with adequate information regarding their plans. Additionally, those individuals that manage the plans (and other fiduciaries) must meet certain standards of conduct, derived from the common law of trusts and made applicable (with certain modifications) to all fiduciaries. The ERISA also contains detailed provisions for reporting to the government and disclosure to participants.

Monitored—Enforced by: The administration of ERISA is divided among the Labor Department, the Internal Revenue Service of the Department of Treasury, and the Pension Benefit Guaranty Corporation (PBGC). Title 1 contains rules for reporting and disclosure, vesting, participation, funding, fiduciary conduct, and civil enforcement, and is administered by the Department of Labor. The ERISA Title II, which amended the Internal Revenue Code to parallel many of the Title I rules, is administered by the IRS. Title III is concerned with jurisdictional matters and with coordination of enforcement and regulatory activities by the Department of Labor and the IRS. Title IV covers the insurance of defined benefit pension plans and is administered by the PBGC.

Year enacted/amended: 1974/1986

• FAIR CREDIT REPORTING ACT (FCRA)

What does the law do? The purpose of the FCRA is to require Consumer Reporting Agencies (CRA) to adopt reasonable procedures for meeting the needs of commerce for consumer credit, personnel, employment, insurance, and other information in a manner which is fair and equitable to the consumer, with regard to the confidentiality, accuracy, relevancy, and proper utilization of such information in accordance with the requirements of this title. Note that the amended law does not apply just to credit reports as is commonly thought. Also note that CRAs are not just credit bureaus. Any organization that issues a report on a consumer is a CRA.

Monitored—Enforced by: Compliance with the requirements imposed under this title shall be enforced under the Federal Trade Commission Act by the Federal Trade Commission with respect to consumer reporting agencies and all other persons subject under the title, except to the extent that enforcement of the requirements imposed under this title is specifically committed to some other government agency.

Year enacted/amended: 1970/1999

• FAIR LABOR STANDARDS ACT (FLSA)

What does the law do? The FLSA provided for minimum standards for both wages and overtime entitlement, and lists the administrative procedures by which covered worktime must be compensated. Also included in the FLSA are provisions for child labor and equal pay.

Monitored—Enforced by: The Wage and Hour Division in the Employment Standards Administration of the Department of Labor administers the FLSA for private employers, state and local governments, the Library of Congress, the United States Postal Service, the Postal Rate Commission, and the Tennessee Valley Authority. The U.S. Equal Employment Opportunity Commission administers the equal pay provisions of the FLSA. The U.S. Office of Personnel Management administers the FLSA provisions with respect to any person employed by a Federal agency.

Year enacted/amended: 1938/2000

• FAMILY AND MEDICAL LEAVE ACT (FMLA)

What does the law do? The FMLA provides certain employees with up to 12 workweeks of unpaid, job-protected leave a year, and requires group health benefits to be maintained during the leave as if employees continued to work instead of taking leave. The act applies to all: public agencies, including state, local and federal employers, local education agencies (schools) private-sector employers who employed 50 or more employees in 20 or more workweeks in the current or preceding calendar year and who are engaged in commerce or in any industry or activity affecting commerce - including joint employers and successors of covered employers.

Monitored—Enforced by: U.S. Department of Labor, Employment Standards Administration, Wage and Hour Division.

Year enacted/amended: 1993/1995

• OCCUPATIONAL SAFETY AND HEALTH ADMINISTRATION (OSHA)

The Occupational Safety and Health Act of 1970 established the Occupational Safety and Health Administration (OSHA) in the U.S. Department of Labor. The primary purpose of the OSHA Act is to provide, so far as possible, every working person in the nation safe and healthful working conditions. Some of the major responsibilities under the OSHA are as follows:

- Employers are responsible for providing their employees a workplace free from recognized hazards that may cause death or serious harm;
- Employers must comply with standards, record keeping, and reporting requirements, and
- Each employee is responsible for his or her own personal safety by complying with the OSHA Act.

In fiscal year 2001, OSHA has a staff of 2,370 including 1,170 inspectors and a budget of $426 million. Sharing the responsibility for oversight of workplace safety and health are 26 states that run their own OSHA programs with 2,948 employees and 1,275 inspectors. Monitored—Enforced by: The Department of Labor is responsible for the enforcement of the Act. This is accomplished through its inspectors and its own internal review procedures. If, however, a decision of the Administration is disputed the case is then forwarded to the Occupational Safety and Health Review Commission. The Commission is an independent, quasi-judicial agency established by the Act and is charged with ruling on cases forwarded to it by the DOL. The Commission is more of a court system than a simple tribunal, for within the Commission there are two levels of adjudication. All cases that require a hearing are assigned to an administrative law judge, who decides the case. Ordinarily the hearing is held in the community where the alleged violation occurred or as close as possible. At the hearing the Secretary of Labor will generally have the burden of proving the case. After the hearing the judge will issue a decision, based on the findings of fact and conclusions of law. A substantial number of the decisions of the judges become final orders of the Commission. However, each decision is subject to discretionary review by the three members of the Commission upon the direction of any one of the three, if done within 30 days of the filing of the decision. When that occurs, the Commission issues its own decision. Once a case is decided, any person adversely affected or aggrieved may obtain a review of the decision in the United States Courts of Appeals.

Year enacted/amended: 1970

• REHABILITATION ACT (RA)

What does the law do? The Rehabilitation Act was the first "rights" legislation to prohibit discrimination against people with disabilities. However, this law applies to programs conducted by Federal agencies, those receiving federal funds, such as colleges participating in federal student loan programs, Federal employment, and employment practices of businesses with federal contracts. The standards for determining employment discrimination under this act are the same as those used in Title I of the Americans with Disabilities Act.

Monitored—Enforced by: The enforcement and compliance of the act are shared with several Federal departments or agencies such as: the Office of Federal Contract Compliance Programs in the U.S. Department of Labor; the Disability Rights Section, Civil Rights Division of the U.S. Department of Justice; and the Equal Employment Opportunity Commission.

Year enacted/amended: 1973/1998

- **UNIFORMED SERVICES EMPLOYMENT AND REEMPLOYMENT RIGHTS ACT (USERRA)**

What does the law do? The USERRA prohibits discrimination against persons because of their service in the Armed Forces Reserve, the National Guard, or other uniformed services. USERRA prohibits an Employer from denying any benefit of employment on the basis of an individual's membership, application for membership, performance of service, application for service, or obligation for service in the uniformed services. The act also protects the rights of veterans, reservists, National Guard members, and certain other members of the uniformed services to reclaim their civilian employment after being absent due to military service or training.

Monitored—Enforced by: The U.S. Office of Special Counsel is authorized by the USERRA to investigate alleged violations of the act by Federal executive agencies, and to prosecute meritorious claims before the Merit Systems Protection Board (MSPB) on behalf of the aggrieved person. All other claims of alleged violations must be filed with the Department of Labor's Veterans' Employment and Training Service (VETS).

Year enacted/amended: 1994

- **THE HEALTH INSURANCE PORTABILITY AND ACCOUNTABILITY (HIPAA)**

The Health Insurance Portability and Accountability Act (HIPAA) provides rights and protections for participants and beneficiaries in group health plans. HIPAA includes protections for coverage under group health plans that limit exclusions for preexisting conditions; prohibit discrimination against employees and dependents based on their health status; and allow a special opportunity to enroll in a new plan to individuals in certain circumstances. HIPAA may also give consumers a right to purchase individual coverage if they have no group health plan coverage available, and have exhausted COBRA or other continuation coverage.

Although the privacy rule took effect in April, 2001, the majority of entities subject to HIPAA have until April 14, 2003 to be in compliance with the rule. Entities qualifying as "small health plans" (those with $5 million or less in annual receipts), have until April 14, 2004 to be in compliance.

The fundamental premise behind HIPAA is that individually identifiable health information created by or received from a covered entity becomes "protected health information." Once protected, the information may only be used by the covered entity for the purposes of patient treatment, payment of health care costs and for health care operations. Other uses must be specifically authorized by the patient. In other words, the HIPAA privacy rule prevents the unauthorized disclosure of a patient's health information without that patient's consent.

Violations of HIPAA's privacy rule provide for both civil and criminal penalties. Sanctions include civil fines of up to $25,000 per year for each violation and fines of up to $250,000 and 10 years imprisonment for the knowing misuse of PHI. DHHS' Office of Civil Rights is in charge of compliance reviews and complaint investigations.

For more information go to: *http://www.dol.gov/ebsa/newsroom/fshipaa.html*

• FREEDOM OF INFORMATION ACT (FOIA)

The Freedom of Information Act *(FOIA)*, is found in Title 5 of the United States Code, Section 552. It was enacted in 1966 and provides that any person has the right to request access to federal agency records. The FOIA does not, however, provide a right of access to records held by state or local government agencies or private businesses or individuals. All documents and records in the possession of the Employee Benefits Security Administration may be available under the Freedom of Information Act. Written requests should specify the document needed and be addressed to the FOIA Disclosure Officer in the appropriate EBSA office. Like all federal agencies, the Department of Labor (DOL) is required under the Freedom of Information Act to disclose records requested in writing by any person. However, agencies may withhold information pursuant to nine exemptions and three exclusions contained in the statute.

NOTES

NOTES

NOTES